D1105808

JOACHIM OF FIORE

JOACHIM OF FIORE

A Study in Spiritual Perception and History

DELNO C. WEST
AND
SANDRA ZIMDARS-SWARTZ

INDIANA UNIVERSITY PRESS

BLOOMINGTON

Manufactured in the United States of America

Library of Congress Cataloging in Publication Data

West, Delno C., 1936–
    Joachim of Fiore.

    Bibliography: p.
    Includes index.
    1. Joachim, of Fiore, ca. 1132–1202.
I. Zimdars-Swartz, Sandra, 1949–   .   II. Title.
BX4705.J6W46   1983   230'.2'0924   81-48635
ISBN 0-253-33179-X
1 2 3 4 5 87 86 85 84 83

1-10-85 jl

To our spouses
Jean M. West
and
Paul Zimdars-Swartz

Without their patience, encouragement, and love,
this book would have not been possible.

Contents

Acknowledgments

Delno C. West wishes to thank Northern Arizona University for research funding; this investigation was supported by the Northern Arizona University Organized Research Fund.

Sandra Zimdars-Swartz wishes to express her sincere thanks to the University of Kansas for support from the General Research Fund, Allocation #3587-20-0038. This support enabled her to revise materials from her dissertation for inclusion in the present work as Chapters III, IV, and V.

Special recognition is due to Robert Maloy, Director of the Smithsonian Institution Libraries (Washington, D.C.), who first guided Zimdars-Swartz in her dissertation and who has continued as a friend and advisor to her and her interests in Joachim of Fiore and his thought.

Lastly, our secretaries, Louise James and Sharon Jones, deserve the highest gratitude for the tedious work and long hours spent on the typescript.

Introduction

In the human mind, history is that which is remembered and that which is expected. In itself, history knows no barriers, no distinguishable ages, or periods. Periodization is an invention of the historian which enables him to categorize the past, select and analyze portions of it, and otherwise deal with it in manageable segments. History is continuous from beginning to end. History is an inquiry into the past, and as such, is useful for modern man. In the Middle Ages, however, the usefulness of inquiry into the past was not considered of particular importance for the reason that the medieval mind did not regard history as a source of significant knowledge. Significant knowledge was that knowledge which led to a fuller understanding of God. For example, Robert Grosseteste, the thirteenth-century English bishop, studied optical science because the Bible said that God is light.

Although it was the most important book to be read during the Middle Ages, the Holy Bible was not regarded as a source for history. The Bible's stories required settings, but the settings themselves were not integral to the stories' implications. Instead, the Bible was a drama of salvation; the scenes paradigms for Christian life applicable to any age. History, on the other hand, was "received"; that is, it was a known quantity and quality. Inquiry into history by a curious mind was counterproductive for medieval men "knew" what had happened in the past, or should have happened. Such an attitude occasionally led to well-intentioned men forging documents, but in light of the prevailing attitude, not malicious; rather, forgery was simply the "modern" record of what everyone knew had happened. History written by the ancients was useful as it supported that which was known. The Bible taught how life should have been, should be, and will be.

To appreciate fully the significance of Joachim of Fiore's contributions, the historical state of mind before and during his time must be understood. The importance of Joachim of Fiore is that he considered inquiry into history as another path to knowing God. He sensed that historical inquiry would provide the key which unlocked hidden meaning in

Scripture, not only to understand the past, but to interpret the future. The Old Testament and New Testament were parallel halves of history which corresponded in significant detail so that the astute observer and reader could extend these parallels and correspondences into the time from the Resurrection to the twelfth century and into the future.

Joachim was first and foremost an exegete and theologian. He had a gifted mind and, as he himself believed, a mind that lifted curtains enabling him to arrive at a more complete understanding of Scripture. His *"spiritualis intelligentia,"* was his deep understanding of the importance of historical inquiry. With an historical sense, he unlocked Scripture previously regarded as confusing, unknowable, or misunderstood.

Joachim's place in the history of apocalyptic interpretation is that of breaking with tradition. The Tichonian-Augustinian view that the Millennium had begun with Christ's first coming and would last until the end of the world, that the New Jerusalem was in reality the Church in its present state beginning at Christ's death, had dominated Christian thought for nearly seven hundred years. Any "New Age" was seen as beyond the dimension of human time. Thus, although several early medieval commentaries on the Apocalypse were produced, notably by Primasius, Bede, Ambrose and Berengarius, they showed little originality from the church fathers.[1] The Tichonian anagogic principle of interpretation dominated. Prophetic symbols and chronologic sequences and events were seen as general truths of the faith. As Ernesto Buonaiuti pointed out early in this century, Joachim's thought was a "complete renascence of the apocalyptic spirit with which the early Christian generations were saturated."[2]

The strength of Joachim's revolutionary new interpretation is to be found in his own visionary powers. He believed very strongly that God had given him "new eyes" with which to comprehend the mysteries of apocalyptic Scripture. *Spiritualis intelligentia* was not in itself a new concept for Biblical interpretation, but the way in which Joachim used this special insight to understand the complexities of symbols and themes of apocalyptic Scripture was.

Without oversimplifying Joachim's exegetical genius, the basic ideas for his eschatological schemata are to be found in St. John the Divine's book itself. The Apocalypse exposes the fundamental laws which govern Christendom and the principles by which any era of history may be judged. Most importantly, St. John had a unity of thought and style that necessitated that the reader-interpreter view the Apocalypse as a whole.

Introduction

The Apocalypse is a work of grandeur—inspired, revealed, and replete with imagery and symbolism. It is genius at work, and genius inspires genius. In the final analysis, the Apocalypse contains the fate of humanity.

Professor Marjorie Reeves in her great study of Joachite imagery, shows Joachim to have had a kaleidoscopic imagination,[3] an imagination which intuitively translated schema, symbols, charts, concordances, and figures into principles of organization as did St. John the Divine. In the twelfth century, a meeting of like minds occurred—St. John the Divine and Joachim of Fiore.

Perhaps Joachim and St. John thought alike because both had a deep sense of history and a philosophy of history. At any rate, the Apocalypse is the only book in the New Testament primarily dedicated to the meaning of history and Joachim understood that. With Joachim seeing the Apocalypse as the fate of mankind, we enter into the twofold realm of history: the remembered past and the expected future. The insight of Joachim is simply that, by a careful analysis of past events and characters, by identifying the parallels and by selectively comparing them, he felt that he had found the key to future expectations as outlined in Holy Scripture.

Abbeviations

DAF   *De articulis fidei.* Edited by E. Buonaiuti, in *Scritti minori di Gioacchino da Fiore.* Rome, 1936.

EA   *Expositio in Apocalypsim.* Venice, 1527. Reprint edition, Frankfurt/M., 1964.

LC   *Liber Concordie novi ac veteris Testamenti.* Venice, 1519. Reprint edition, Frankfurt/M., 1964.

PDC   *Psalterium decem chordarum.* Venice, 1527. Reprint edition, Frankfurt/M., 1965.

STA   "Short Tract on the Apocalypse." Edited by J. Huck under the titles *Enchiridion in Apocalypsim* and *De titulo libri Apocalypsi,* in *Joachim von Floris und die joachitische Literatur,* Freiburg im Breisgau, 1938, pp. 287–296.

TSQE   *Tractatus super Quatuor Evangelia.* Edited by E. Buonaiuti, Rome, 1930.

VSB   *De vita sancti Benedicti et de officio divino secundum ejus doctrinam.* Edited by C. Baraut in "Un tratado inedito de Joaquin de Fiore," *Analecta sacra tarraconensia* 24 (1951), pp. 22-122.

JOACHIM
OF FIORE

CHAPTER I

The Life of
Joachim of Fiore

T HE two primary sources of knowledge about Joachim of Fiore's
life are the biographies left to us by Joachim's secretary, Luke
of Cosenza, *Virtutum Beati Joachimi synopsis*, and the anony-
mous *Vita beati Joachimi abbatis*.[1] A few autobiographical
facts can be gleaned from Joachim's writings, primarily his testamentary
letter, *Epistola prologasis*, written in 1200 to the abbots of his Order of
St. John of Fiore. Other incidents are recorded in various chronicles, such
as those by Fra Salimbene of Parma and Ralph of Coggeshall, and in
apocryphal legends of the times.

In the seventeenth century, Jocobus Graecus Syllanous, a monk at
Fiore, produced a narrative of Joachim's life. This narrative listed the
supposed miracles of Joachim and may have relied on documents, no
longer extant, which were compiled during the fourteenth century effort
to canonize Joachim. Gregorius de Laude also produced a *Vita* in the seventeenth century which is nearly identical to that of Jocobus Graecus.
Both Jocobus Graecus and Gregorius de Laude drew heavily from the
Virtutum Beati Joachimi synopsis and the *Vita beati Joachimi abbatis*.
Most modern biographical efforts are based on these narratives. As with
most religious figures, early biographical sources are filled with common
legends, anecdotes, and other stories promoting the saintliness of the character. Consequently, very little is known of the details of the Calabrian
monk's life.

Joachim of Fiore was born at Celico in the diocese of Cosenza in the
region of Calabria, Italy, about A.D. 1135. He died in 1202. His father was
Mauro the Notary who held a bureaucratic office at the court of Roger II
of Sicily. Joachim began his career by following in his father's service to
the Sicilian court. Outside of one trip to Constantinople and the Holy
Lands while in the king's service, Joachim lived out his life in southern

1

Italy, rarely venturing from Corazzo or his beloved wilderness of the Sila Mountains in Calabria.

Calabria was a harsh countryside, wild and desolate. Geographically and politically, the province was more closely associated with Sicily than with the Italian peninsula. Historically, it had been more Greek than Latin, and from the mid-eleventh century, Calabria was a part of the Norman holdings. Culturally this territory was extremely complex. The population was Latin, Lombard, Norman, and Greek. The Muslim influence was strong, particularly in government. In Calabria, Greek was spoken and Greek Orthodox Christianity was dominant in both church and monastery. The Norman rulers maintained an enlightened policy of tolerance toward Jews, Greeks, and Saracens alike, local rights and usages were protected. Greek and Muslim learning and artistic achievements were recognized and patronized under numerous Norman kings.

Politically, the Norman kingdom was the most sophisticated in Europe. Public administration was carried out by bureaucratic specialists recruited by talent rather than feudal birth. The king ruled through a political system designed after the Byzantine. Documents were issued in Greek and Arabic as well as Latin in a format copied from the Byzantine and papal courts.

By the twelfth century, southern Italy and the Norman holdings had become prime targets in the territorial conflicts between the Pope and the Holy Roman Emperor. The Emperor Frederick Barbarossa was able to arrange a marriage between his son, Henry, and Constance, the heiress of King William II's throne in southern Italy and Sicily. This alliance seemed to assure that the region would fall under the hegemony of the Empire.

Yet, the unification was not easily forthcoming. In southern Italy and Sicily, a party opposed to this arrangement raised Tancred of Lecce to the throne when William II died and aligned itself with the Papacy. This situation received full support from Richard I of England. The Hohenstaufen Emperor, Henry VI, was thus forced into an Italian campaign from 1191 to 1194.

In the end, the Holy Roman Empire was triumphant due to the capture of Richard I by Duke Leopold of Austria and the death of Tancred in 1194. Finally, on Christmas Day, 1194, Henry VI was crowned King of Sicily, Apulia, and Calabria.

Although Joachim spent most of his life somewhat isolated in southern Italy in monasteries or as a hermit, he could not totally avoid the events which raged around him. Joachim's one major journey was important to his final career. Early in his court service, he was sent with an official party to Constantinople by King William I, the Bad. William had recently completed peace agreements with the Byzantine Emperor Manuel I Comnenus and this trip probably was to negotiate further with the Byzantine government.

Joachim was in his early or mid-twenties. For reasons which are unclear, he left William's service while in Constantinople, and instead journeyed to the Holy Lands in search of God's will in his life. There, according to legend, Joachim felt a special call from God while wandering in the Palestine desert. After this experience, he spent the Lenten season meditating on Mount Tabor. Joachim implied in the *Expositio in Apocalypsim* that on the eve of Easter day, he received "the fullness of knowledge" toward the end of his stay on the mountain.[2]

The young convert did not return immediately to Calabria, instead he spent some time as a hermit near Mt. Etna in Sicily. After a while, he became a wandering preacher reentering Calabria as an independent religious. He settled as a visitor in the Cistercian monastery, Sambucina. As he would note later in life, the independent preacher's life was subject to spiritual pitfalls and he was totally against such an occupation. While at Sambucina, he traveled to the bishop of Catanzaro in order to be ordained. Shortly thereafter, Joachim became a monk and entered the Benedictine monastery, Corazzo, where he would eventually become abbot and lead the monks of Corazzo to follow the Cistercian rules.

Luke of Cosenza describes Joachim as a humble and kindly man of extraordinary devotion. Luke tells us that Joachim was given mostly to study and prayer, that he wore the oldest, shabbiest clothes he could find, and that he was a poor sleeper, resting only a few hours a night. He was prone to go without meals. Nevertheless, despite Joachim's seeming disregard for his health, he was, according to Luke, strong and robust.

Luke emphasized Joachim's humbleness and devotion. Whenever he could, Joachim would perform the lowest tasks of the monastery such as bedmaking, cooking, or scrubbing the infirmary floor. It was Luke who assisted Joachim with the Mass, and Luke was unusually impressed with the intensity with which Joachim celebrated the service. Joachim was reported to be an excellent preacher who tended to begin his sermons in a low voice, but who soon would resound "like thunder."[3]

Joachim's humbleness can also be illustrated in his attitude toward those who persecuted him. Fra Salimbene records for us how the refectorer of Corazzo disliked Joachim and daily for a full year filled Joachim's drinking vessel with water instead of wine. Such petty abuse Joachim "bore with patience and without complaint." Finally, this abuse came to light when during the one meal the monks shared with the abbot, the abbot insisted that Joachim share his wine with him. The abbot was furious when he tasted the water and forced Joachim to explain why his vessel contained water instead of wine. The abbot was inclined to discipline and dismissed the refectorer immediately, but Joachim intervened by declaring that "water is a sober drink which neither ties the tongue nor brings about drunkenness, nor makes men babble!"[4] Actually, Joachim was quite serious about this as he recommends later in his career that wine was not a proper drink for monks.[5]

Joachim, well-liked by both his superiors and his peers, rose rapidly to prior and then to abbot of Corazzo in 1178. Joachim did not wish to be abbot nor did he enjoy the job after he was appointed. Several influential churchmen, including the Archbishop of Cosenza, had to convince him to accept the post. Administrative details and the laxity of the lives of his monks kept him from his real mission and love—the recording of the multitude of ideas, visions, symbols, and figures which floated in his mind.

Within five years, Joachim was neglecting the leadership of his monastery. He left Corazzo for the abbey of Casamari where he virtually cloistered himself in 1183 for over a year to begin his great trilogy: *Liber Concordie novi ac veteris Testamenti* (Harmony of the New and Old Testaments), *Expositio in Apocalypsim* (Exposition of Apocalypse), and *Psalterium decem chordarum* (Psaltery of Ten Strings). Although he spent the rest of his life refining these writings, this initial period was so productive that he kept Luke and two other monks busy day and night writing his dictation and making corrections of the manuscripts. At times all three works were in progress simultaneously. With the exhaustive project underway, Joachim traveled to see Pope Lucius in 1184 to seek release from his administrative duties. Pope Lucius had Joachim's unfinished *Liber Concordie novi ac veteris Testamenti* studied, and after the reading, encouraged Joachim to continue his writing. He released Joachim from his office as abbot. Joachim returned to Corazzo and for the next few years continued to write his commentaries. In 1188, Pope Clement III again encouraged Joachim in his efforts and asked that the final product be examined by the papal curia when it was finished.

Joachim left Corazzo for good in 1189. He and a close friend, Ranier, journeyed to the mountains of Pietralata. There they lived for a time as hermits in cells. It proved impossible for Joachim to remain in seclusion, however, for he and Ranier were soon joined by others wishing a stricter religious life. The result was the foundation of St. John of Fiore Abbey on Mt. Nero.

Joachim and his followers were isolated in the wild mountainous countryside of Pietralata; nevertheless, they were not able to avoid the outside world. Throughout 1192–1193, the new monastery was ravaged by the forces of church and state as each tried to establish control over the region. Also, a nearby Greek Orthodox monastery quarreled with Joachim and his monks over pasturage rights. The quarrel culminated in an attack upon St. John of Fiore by the Greek monks and portions of the new buildings were burned.

The Order of St. John of Fiore received gifts and privileges from Tancred of Lecce in 1195, and from the Emperor Henry VI and his wife, Constance, shortly thereafter. On April 25, 1196, Pope Celestine III issued a bull approving the new Order.[6] Confirmation of that approval was issued in another bull in 1204 by Innocent III and twice by Honorius in 1216 and 1220. The order grew slowly, perhaps reaching 60 houses in all, and it was not the vanguard for any prophetic thrust promoting its founder's ideas. Basically, the Florensian Order conservatively followed the reforms of the Cistercians. Three hundred years later, in 1505, most of the order united with the Cistercians, while other Florensian houses joined the Carthusians or Dominicans.

Joachim's fame as an expositor and prophet spread widely by the end of the twelfth century. During his lifetime, contemporary chroniclers recorded some of his activities and explanations of prophetic Scripture. He visited with three popes and on at least one occasion spoke before Pope Lucius III and the papal curia.[7] Kings sought him out, notably Richard I of England, Philip Augustus of France, and the Emperor Henry VI. After his death in 1202, even while his fame increased, a considerable controversy arose in regard to his significance. Some thought of him as a man of great wisdom, others revered him as a prophet, and still others damned him as a false teacher. His message had special appeal to the new mendicant orders and through their advocacy, Joachim's ideas were rapidly spread northward. Joachim's reputation, however, was damaged by two events in the thirteenth century—the Fourth Lateran Council of 1215 and the special commission established in 1255–1256 to review Joachim's interpretations.

The Fourth Lateran Council condemned Joachim for his supposed criticism of Peter Lombard's doctrine on the Trinity. The tract in question which the council attributed to Joachim is now lost. According to the testimony of the council, Joachim accused Peter Lombard of having defined *"essentia"* in such a way as to imply a fourth member of the Godhead.

More damaging to Joachim's reputation was the scandal over the so-called "Eternal Gospel" advocated by Gerard of Borgo San Donnino. In 1253 or 1254, Gerard, a Franciscan, composed a gloss of Joachim's works prefaced by a *Liber Introductorius*. The document has not survived. Our knowledge of this scandal comes from the testimony of the commission appointed in 1255 to investigate Gerard's work.

The dispute over Gerard of Borgo San Donnino's *Liber Introductorius* and gloss is far more complicated than a brief summary can adequately explain. Gerard got into trouble on three fronts. Gerard did arrive at basic heretical and disobedient conclusions. His promulgation of Joachim's works as an expected third gospel—the "Eternal Gospel"— served to polarize the disputing Franciscan and secular faculty and students at the University of Paris to the point of open confrontation, but most importantly, Gerard was the first student of Joachim's scheme to reach the potentially radical conclusions in regard to the world order that could be drawn from Joachim's three ages of history. Fra Salimbene, who had known Gerard for many years, felt that the friar had simply "gone mad."[8]

In the end, the commission meeting at Anagni condemned the natural conclusion a reader could come to that Joachim's third epoch of the world would replace the authority of the Roman Catholic Church. Later, in 1263, a provincial council at Arles condemned the whole schema of the three epochs as envisioned by Joachim and his followers.

Neither the condemnations by a commission nor by a provincial council are in themselves final acts. Joachim's works were never condemned by a pope or any higher authority than the Anagni Commission. The publicity and notoriety resulting from the investigations, however, raised serious questions about Joachim and his teachings; questions which remain controversial in the scholarly world today.

There are over fifty literary works attributed to or associated with

Joachim of Fiore. Out of this number, perhaps sixteen were written by Joachim himself: the rest are spurious or were written by his disciples. Several modern scholars have attempted to identify exactly which writings were truly Joachim's, a difficult and time-consuming task which continues as many items in the literary corpus remain in question.

The *Liber Concordie novi ac veteris Testamenti, Expositio in Apocalypsim*, and *Psalterium decem chordarum* present a trilogy of purpose and organization for Joachim's major themes. Written and corrected over a period of nearly sixteen years, they form an indisputably integrated community of thought despite differences in subject matter and intention. The author finished his drafts of the *Liber Concordie novi ac veteris Testamenti* and the *Expositio in Apocalypsim* before beginning the *Psalterium decem chordarum* while revising the other two, and he cross-referenced ideas among all three books whenever he felt it necessary. To him, the three works were inseparable and meant to be read as a whole.

The *Liber Concordie novi ac veteris Testamenti* was first in time and order, and it set the style and scene for the other works. In this elaborate parallel of the Old Testament and New Testament, Joachim tried to point out the correspondence of each person, event, and period to be found in the Old Testament with a person, event, or period in the New Testament. Then the correspondences were shown to prefigure similar persons, events, and periods in the third and final age of human history. In essence, the *Liber Concordie novi ac veteris Testamenti* is a grand philosophy of history.

Before the main text of the *Expositio in Apocalypsim*, the abbot included a "Prologue" and "Introduction." The prologue was a justification for his publications in which he warned his readers that his comments were not to be taken lightly. He did not set out presumptuously but with papal authority and blessing. Indeed, at the onset, he instructed the monks of his abbey to deliver his writings to the Holy See immediately should he die before they were finished. In the "Introduction," Joachim summarized his major ideas about the three ages, the seven seals, and the concord between the two Testaments.

In the *Expositio in Apocalypsim*, Joachim goes into great detail to explain fully the symbols, visions, and figures of the *Apocalypse*. Since Joachim considered the *Apocalypse* to be the key to understanding all Scripture, the *Expositio in Apocalypsim* is essential to all of Joachim's biblical exegesis.

As Joachim edited these two great treatises, he feared that he still had not totally clarified his view of the Trinity. He tells us that after earnest prayer, there appeared in his mind the figure of the ten-stringed psaltery (or lyre) which would represent the Trinity. The *Psalterium decem chordarum* is an allegorical presentation of Joachim's notion of three historical stages. The body of the instrument represents the Father; the psalms sung with the aid of the instrument represent the Son; and the melody produced by both the instrument and the singing represents the Holy Spirit.

When Joachim died in 1202, he was preparing a fourth book regarded by modern scholars as an integral part of the abbot's major expository plan. The *Tractatus super Quatuor Evangelia* was written to be understood within Joachim's scheme of history as outlined in his other major works. The four Gospels are presented to us as progressive consummations of historical periods that culminate with the eternal Sabbath after the end of history.

Joachim composed a number of minor tracts, letters, poems, and sermons on topics both relevant and non-relevant to his apocalyptic theology. Of these, mention should be made of the *Adversus Iudaeos* in which Joachim wished to prepare the Jews for their inevitable conversion expected at the beginning of the third age.

Although extensive research has been done on the famous *Liber Figurarum*, it remains controversial in authorship. It may have been drawn and written by Joachim, by someone under his direction, or by someone totally outside his direct influence. This book of illustrations, with few exceptions, presents visual images which relate to Joachim's main ideas. This book was extremely important to the spread of Joachim's thought throughout Europe.

Throughout the thirteenth century, and even later, many compositions were attributed to Joachim of Fiore so that pseudo-Joachim works proliferated into a large corpus of their own. The most famous of these were the *Super Hieremiam, Super Esaiam*, and *De Septem Sigillis*. Unfortunately, much of Joachim's early reputation derived from these spurious works, especially those which related contemporary events to his apocalyptic themes.

We know few details of Joachim's life and scholars are still attempting to arrive at an exact corpus of his literature. A monk from Southern Italy who knew kings and emperors and popes; a Cistercian who broke from his order and established a more stringent rule; a visionary exegete of

8

apocalyptic Scripture who challenged the church fathers in his interpretations; an abbot whose writings were frequently suspect but were never condemned by the Holy See; a holy man who was never sainted but who was placed by Dante in the circle of the Sun next to St. Bonaventura and St. Francis in the *Paradiso*. Joachim has been hailed as a proto-Renaissance figure, yet some of his most vocal supporters were reactionary and extremist elements in the thirteenth and fourteenth centuries. Frank Manuel, in his study, *Shapes of Philosophical History*, comes close to the true picture of Joachim of Fiore when he advocates that Joachim was "heir to the exegetical, tropological, allegorical and numerological traditions of the church fathers. These he fashioned into a symbolism uniquely his own, which he placed in the service of a new world history."[9]

CHAPTER II

The Basic Patterns and Interpretations of Joachim of Fiore

J OACHIM OF FIORE'S major contribution to learning was to conceive a spiritual perception of history. Through a study of biblical concordances, he concluded that one could understand the impelling force of God's design that led through Jesus Christ to an historical consummation that was still in the future. The purpose of God and his design of history could be found only in the written dispensations of Holy Scripture, which to Joachim contained an exact revelation of God's purpose. Since God was clearly the *primum mobile* in control of the universe, everything past and future served God's ultimate plan. This observation essentially meant that history has a meaning and direction that can be seen only if Scripture could be interpreted accurately.

Reflecting on various clues he found in Scripture, Joachim arrived at the conclusion that history is divided into three "Epochs" which have rather clear-cut chronological termini. Further, he believed that the Advent of Christ, the single most important event in God's scheme, was at the center of history. It was the pivot around which all events swung. Christ's birth, life, and passion were the most essential facts of history, and his return would signal its consummation. Stages of development, or epochs, are consequently self-evident: a period before Christ, a period after Christ, and a period yet in the future that would be eschatological in nature. The first epoch was simple to map out; it proceeded from Adam to Christ. The beginning of the next epoch was similarly easy; it began with Christ. The end of the second epoch and beginning of the third, however, could not yet be determined although Joachim found many indications of the closeness of its beginning.

Many books of the Bible are eschatological and apocalyptic. Old Testament writings such as Daniel and the New Testament Gospel of John prepare the reader for the final book, the Apocalypse. This vision uses images, symbolic language, and mystical numbers to show the Last Days when a series of crises will precede the Advent of the New Jerusalem and the final triumph of Christian believers. After terrible tribulations destroy secular powers, the earthly reign of Christ will begin and continue for a thousand years. After this Millennium, Antichrist will be loosed in one last great convulsion before God appears to conclude world history and establish an eternal state of peace.

The interpretation of these prophetic scriptures was a popular theme of early medieval writers. Gregory the Great, Beatus of Liebana, Bede, and Adso are to be found among important thinkers who addressed themselves to this fascinating topic. All this interpretation, however, had been cast early on by Tichonius and St. Augustine into a non-chiliastic mold. There was little variation from this tradition until Joachim of Fiore broke sharply with it.

Tichonius (d.c. A.D. 400) was a man of great learning who wrote a treatise on the Apocalypse of St. John that is no longer extant. Enough was quoted from Tichonius' commentary by later authors, though, to make his position fairly well understood. He believed that the Apocalypse did not address itself so much to future events as to the general attacks of diabolical forces upon the Church. Tichonius' premise was that Christ and Satan were two great powers struggling for mastery of the earth. The New Jerusalem was not an expected event in world history; rather, it was the present Church, which came into existence upon Christ's death and extended through time to the end of days. Tichonius accordingly composed seven rules for interpreting the Apocalypse which were adopted with minor variation by St. Augustine. It became the standard within which subsequent expositors worked.[1]

St. Augustine (d. A.D. 430) popularized Tichonius' rules to such an extent that the chiliastic expectations of early Christians lost all currency. Under the influence of St. Augustine's theology, allegorical biblical interpretation became so dominant it was the only standard for Christian exegetes. He also developed a world-week chronology based on the six days of creation. These time periods were not to be seen as literal but as phases of creation symbolizing the ages of history. These periods were: (1) Adam to Noah, (2) Noah to Abraham, (3) Abraham to David, (4) David to the Captivity, (5) The Captivity to Christ, (6) Christ to the End of History, (7) The Second Advent and Eternal Rest.

11

The startling focus of St. Augustine's argument was that the Millennium of Apocalypse 20 had already begun with the Advent of Christ and would end with His second coming. Following the six-day pattern of creation laid down in Genesis 1, St. Augustine saw the present historical period was the sixth age. At the end of the sixth period, the Antichrist would be set loose for three and one-half years to cause tribulation for mankind. The final Sabbath period would be spiritual and beyond the dimension of human history. To St. Augustine, the historical trend was one of deterioration. His vision was that of a more perfect age in the past and of another yet to come. He was living in an age sure to decline until the end of world order immediately preceding the Second Advent. He focused on the Kingdom as a then-present reality on earth that had begun with the First Advent.

Joachim's addition to this vision was a fresh focus on a new world order, one to be ushered in with a New Age of guidance by the Holy Spirit acting through a new order of meditative men who truly contemplated God. This age would be followed by the Second Advent and a period of peace and tranquility.

Tichonius and St. Augustine viewed the Apocalypse of St. John as instructional instead of prophetic. Joachim of Fiore turned this moral view to an historical view within the tradition of the primitive church, which had expected a thousand-year period of bliss as the culmination of history and time.

An even more innovative aspect of Joachim's writings was his interpretation of the mission of the Holy Spirit. The church fathers had conceived the Holy Spirit as the force which developed and spread the teachings of Christ. Joachim, on the other hand, held that the Holy Spirit would complete the teachings of Christ and unlock God's last revelation before the end of time.[2]

Traditionally, Christians had considered the nature of prophecy to be such as to require symbols to penetrate to the inner meaning of prophetic texts. The ability to use symbolism had been considered a special talent or gift. Joachim, too, believed that he had been blessed with "new eyes" in order to see the true meaning of Scripture. Frequently, the interpreter of prophecy received from God visual insight into the mysteries of Scripture, which, combined with lengthy study, produced for man comprehensive explanations of eschatology. Joachim admittedly relied on God's help. In one passage he tells his readers that the Apocalypse posed insurmountable problems for him until suddenly, on the eve of Easter and after much meditation, he awakened about midnight and "in the night's silence . . . the full understanding of this book [The Apocalypse] and the total agreement of the Old Testament and New Testament was comprehended with clarity of understanding in the eye of my mind."[3]

Joachim's grand schemes are complex and highly detailed, but nonetheless unified.[4] His straightforward, medieval use of numbers, geometric forms, words, and biological phenomena to express his ideas symbolically provides a basic explanation of his scheme. His biological symbolism, althought not unique in the exegeses of Scripture, is ideal to his philosophy of history because trees, flowers, and plant life show most clearly an unfolding, a becoming. He used flora to symbolize the interrelationships of the three status and the dynamic character of history and to indicate the potential of human and institutional development. Seeds, the fledgling growths, the maturing plants, can easily symbolize the full fructification of a species.

Figure I demonstrates this quite clearly. In this famous drawing of Trinitarian Tree Circles, Joachim comprehends all of history. The tree is rooted in Noah and from Noah branches forth three sons—Shem, Japhet, and Ham. Ham and his offspring are removed from history, and his lineage is consequently pictured as a stump, axed almost before it grows, whereas Shem and Japhet become the two great trunks of human history—Jew and Gentile—that circle and cross each other to form the three *status* so important to Joachim's scheme. Around the second circle, representing Christ, the Gentile trunk of Japhet grows more abundantly, and in the third circle, representing the Third Epoch of the Holy Spirit and the period after the conversion of the Jews, full fruition crowns all history.

The fluid growth and motion of the plant points to the essence of Joachim's comprehension of world events. The key to his patterns and interpretations is his assumption that each new age of history comprehends the past within itself. Thus, to Joachim, Scripture taught a record of man's gradual spiritual developments, leading toward a perfected future age which was the fulfillment of prophetic hope. In the vision that came to him after extensive study of Scripture, Joachim conceptualized three basic epochs of human history: those of the Father, of the Son, and of the Holy Spirit. The first epoch had concluded with the Advent of Christ, the second epoch was coming to its end shortly, while the third epoch had been already heralded and would soon be ushered in.

FIGURE I Trinitarian Tree Circles   *Bodleian Library, Oxford University*

The starting point for all of Joachim's ideas is the concordance of the two dispensations (i.e., the Old and New Testaments) in history. From this he envisioned three *status*, or three epochs, of historical development. To Joachim, as to all medieval theologians, concordance was a rigorous method of exegesis measuring one testament by the other. A partial understanding of the meaning of Scripture could result from this comparison. When he applied this method, Joachim found parallel chronologies of history in the concordance between the Old and New Testaments, and a third parallel emerged from his speculations on the first two. There would be a third epoch, yet to come, springing naturally from the other two and following their pattern. Within the first two dispensations, Joachim saw the pattern in play of certain numerical patterns, especially in models of seven, double seven, and twelve.

He further calculated the epoch in terms of the generations of men. He found that each of the first two epochs, which overlapped, contained three sets of 21 generations. These generations gave a more exact chronology and time frame for each age and implied that the third epoch would be similar.

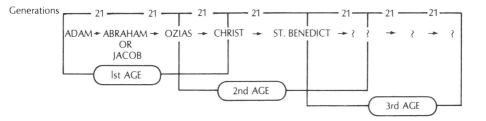

Immediately, the reader is faced with the question of whether Joachim anticipated a third dispensation (or biblical book) to match the third epoch. He had shown the Old and New Testaments as concordant in person, type, and event. For example, the twelve patriarchs corresponded to the twelve disciples; and Caleb, Joshua, and Moses corresponded to Peter, John, and Paul. Yet the New Testament superseded the Old Testament and emanated from it.

Joachim did not postulate a third testament, however. The third epoch would not receive a new text, but rather the Holy Spirit would reveal to the third epoch a special understanding of existing Scripture through the gift of *spiritualis intellectus*. Indeed, in the totality of Joachim's writings, the reader can conclude only that the three epochs are levels of spiritual growth with no anticipation of corresponding testaments. Joachim even states explicitly that no new literature would appear, but that existing texts would become fully known; thus a new interpretation of Scripture and a new form of contemplative worship would evolve.[5]

Much of Joachim's vision centers around number symbolism, which from the earliest times had been seen as an important key to unlocking cosmic secrets. Numbers are one way in which the mind perceives reality as it exists in time and space. Man can sense the traverse of the sun across the sky and the distance from the hill to valley, but the underlying meaning of such phenomena is the province of the intellect. Time is ordered into an unchangeable sequence of units that we can comprehend through our sensual abilities. Yet, the human mind comprehends that beneath time and space there is a more complete reality, and it is to this reality that men have tried to penetrate for centuries. Sensual perception leads to discovery, but the mind leads to understanding.

The Christian faith inherited number hypotheses from various sources, most notably the Egyptian, Mesopotamian, and Greek systems of numerology that had been designed to order the universe into fixed truths. Through the use of number symbolism, early Christian writers conceived a finite and orderly universe. Numerical meaning made accessible to the human mind the ultimate reality after which earthly life could be patterned. Numbers were "the method by which the Divine Intellect becomes intelligible *per enigmatem* to human comprehension."[6]

Joachim integrates these numerological systems into his major divisions of time by using three basic terms for historical reference. In the first instance he divided history into three *status* (the epochs), which connect the members of the Holy Trinity. He used this term "status" only when speaking of the three broad, basic divisions. The second basic term is *tempus*, which he used to subdivide the three *status*. The third usage is *etas*, which he used to divide salvation history into seven time periods, that is, a sevenfold division of time, which cuts across and corresponds to the three status.

It is seen in Figure II (from the *Liber Figurarum*) that the three epochs relate to the Godhead and its work in history. By definition of the ancient councils, the Holy Trinity was a tri-unity, and thus, the number 3 is the number of perfection, the essence of all things. In the deepest sense, the number 3 is a unity unto itself. This is easily demonstrated by the com-

16

pleteness of the entity of the triangle where pairs of opposites are united and harmonized into a third symbol. Joachim could see within this mystical number the diversity which allowed for the dual nature of Christ, the two dispensations, and the dissemination of divine knowledge by the four gospels. In like manner, 3, because of its quality of composition, could be extended to other forms of perfection, such as 7 and 12.

To connect the history of the universe with the triad was not unique with Joachim. St. Augustine had done this in his *City of God*, in which he proclaimed three stages of history; those "Before the Law (Adam to Moses)," "Under the Law (Moses to Christ)," and "Under the Gospel (Christ to the Last Judgment)."[7] Joachim simply applied a direct involvement of each member of the Trinity to each epoch. In the first epoch, the Father worked in mystery through the Patriarchs and the sons of the prophets. In the second epoch, the Son worked through the Apostles and other apostolic men. Joachim foresaw the Holy Spirit working through the religious orders in the third epoch.

Although Joachim's number pattern may seem very similar to St. Augustine's, a striking difference exists. Whereas St. Augustine believed history to be passing through the last age, Joachim believed the last age had not yet arrived. Joachim's own words explain his position:

> The first epoch was that in which we were under the law, the second when we were under grace, the third when we will live in anticipation of even richer grace. . . . The first epoch was in knowledge, the second in the authority of wisdom, the third in the perfection of understanding. The first in the chains of the slave, the second in the service of a son, the third in freedom. The first in exasperation, the second in action, the third in contemplation. The first in fear, the second in faith, the third in love. The first under slave bondage, the second in freedom, the third in friendship. The first the age of children, the second the age of youth, the third that of the old. The first in starlight, the second in moonlight, the third in full daylight. The first in winter, the second in spring, the third in summer. The first the seedling of a plant, the second roses, the third lilies. The first producing grass, the second stalks, the third wheat. The first water, the second wine, the third oil. . . .[8]

Joachim's explanation of these triplets is found in his *Expositio in Apocalypsim*:

> The first of the three epochs spoken of existed during the age of the law. Then the Lord's people . . . were under the elements of this world. They

were unable to attain the liberty of spirit spoken of by the one who said: "If the Son liberates you, you will be free indeed." The second epoch was initiated under the Gospel. It remains to the present with some liberty considered from the perspective of the past but not with the freedom to be characterized in the future. . . . The third epoch, therefore, will be ushered in toward the close of the present age, no longer under the screen of the letter but in the spirit of complete freedom. The first epoch, under the law of circumcision, was begun with Adam. The second, flowering under the Gospel was instituted by Uzziah. The third, based on our calculation of the generations, was heralded by St. Benedict, its consummation of unsurpassed splendor is to be seen near the end. At that time Elias will be revealed and the unbelieving people of the Jews will be converted to the Lord. At that time, the Holy Spirit will appear to cry in a loud voice. "The Father and the Son have worked up to this time, and now I work."[9]

On the role of the dispensations, Joachim continues:

The letter of the former Testament seems properly to pertain to the Father. The letter of the New Testament pertains to the Son. Likewise the spiritual understanding proceeds beyond both Father and Son to the Holy Spirit. . . . In the first epoch, the order of the married prevailed and this seems to pertain to the Father. The order of clerks are the second epoch and likewise, the order of monks, having been established at the very end of the era, pertains to the Holy Spirit. According to this, the first epoch is . . . ascribed to the Father, the second to the Son, the third to the Holy Spirit.[10]

After Joachim envisioned history controlled by the Godhead in three stages, he sought to find parallels, or concordances, between the first two epochs. By implication, and by Joachim's design, each illustration of the concord of the two Testaments was a person or event in world history. The difference in the circumstances was not in kind, but in quality, since the New Testament events had a fuller expression or accomplishment than the Old Testament.

In the *Expositio in Apocalypsim*, Joachim turned to the mystery of numbers other than 3 to explain these events. The number 7 was an extension of the divine quality of the Godhead because within that Godhead is the cross with four points and the four gospels which proclaim divine knowledge. The number 4 traditionally represented the temporal whereas the number 3 traditionally represented the spiritual. Four was the symbol of earthly things because the earth was created on the fourth day, matter was composed of four elements, the earth had four seasons, and the earth contained four cardinal points (directions). In the combination of the numbers 3 and 4, the spiritual and the temporal unite to offer stability in all existence, and Joachim found this an expression of divine guidance in world affairs. To support further the quality of composition contained in 7, Joachim reminds us that the book found in the Apocalypse, Chapters 5–7, is sealed with 7 seals (to Joachim the book was the Old Testament), and that Christ revealed the meaning and harmony of history by opening the seven seals after His Resurrection.[11]

The number 7 implies completion: God ended His work, rested, and blessed the 7th day (Genesis 2:2–3). The number 7, basically a spiritual number, is related to time (e.g., in the week). Rather than depicting space, it portrays evolution and perfection or completion. In Christian thought, time does not have an earthly existence; rather, it has been implanted into the physical world by spiritual powers. This, too, is an idea that can be expressed by the mystic number 7.

Joachim also found the numbers 5 and 12 to be highly significant. The number 5 not only contains in its aggregate the Two Dispensations and the three members of the Trinity, but it relates to man and his destiny in that man has five extremities—head, arms, legs—and 5 senses through which he may perceive evil. By combining 5 and 7, Joachim concluded that 12 was the foundation number which fulfills prophecy. Five is the promise, 7 is the action, and 12 is the fulfillment. The inheritance of the 12 tribes of Israel, for example, was received first by 5 tribes and then by the other 7. The first five major churches in the New Testament were soon followed by the seven churches of Asia Minor.[12] And, there are 5 senses and 7 spiritual gifts which combine within the person to furnish Christian fulfillment.

Based on these patterns, Joachim built his schema in which the number 5 represented the Second Epoch and 7 represented the third Epoch. Twelve is significant to both Old Testament and New Testament numerology, and Joachim frequently points to concordances of twelves. In the Old Testament, for example, there are 12 patriarchs, 12 tribes, and 12 jewels in the breast plate of the high priest. In the New Testament, there are 12 apostles, 12 gates in the New Jerusalem, and 12 was the age of Christ when he was found by Joseph and Mary in the Temple. Twelve is also the sign of universality when the spiritual 3 and the temporal 4 are multiplied.

19

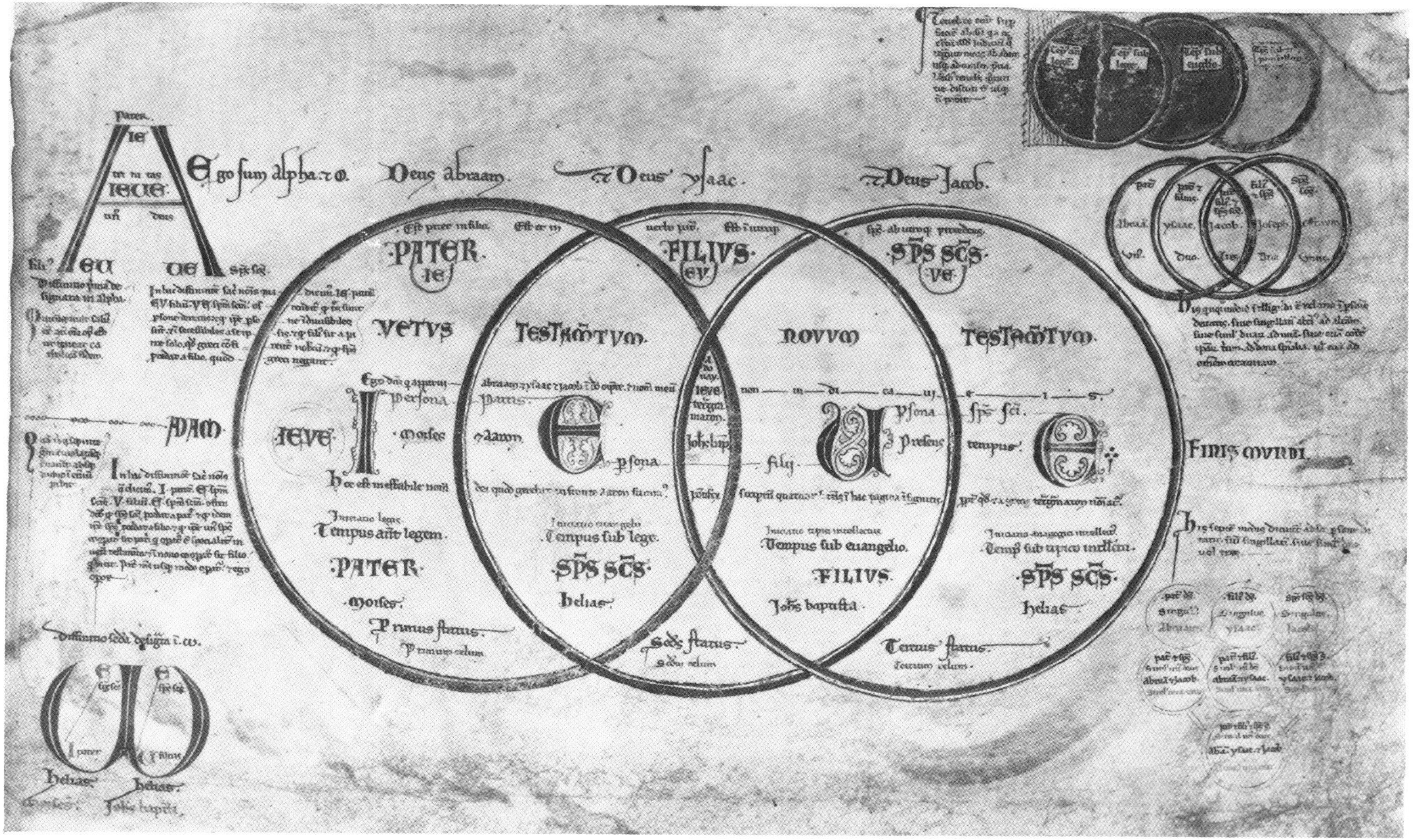

FIGURE II Trinitarian Circles

Bodleian Library, Oxford University

In the Bodleian Ms. of the *Liber Figurarum*, Figure II is shown as a colored geometrical diagram which corresponds to the number symbolism outlined above. The circle (which symbolizes eternity) of the Father is drawn in green, which indicates hope. In pagan symbolism, green meant the coming of spring and unripe fruit. The circle of the Son is blue, which signifies monarchy and heaven or, as in this case, the Christ as king of the universe. The circle of the Holy Spirit is displayed in red to signify the passion of Christ, love, and ripe fruit—or the fulfillment of the planting cycle.

Scholars have yet to study the use of color in the *Liber Figurarum* drawings. A cursory glance at the major colors used seems to imply a definite purpose and a selectivity of color beyond the aesthetic. For example, brown and pink are frequently intertwined with these colors of green, blue, and red. Brown indicates both the temporality of the earth and the renunciation of earthly things. The brown monastic clothing, for example, indicates penitence and poverty. Pink is associated with the same qualities associated with the number 5. In Joachim's grand scheme, the third epoch will be one of contemplation led by a new monastic order of men.

Joachim defines the parallel concordances of the Old Testament and the New Testament in seven stages, and then projects the meanings of these stages on the seven seals of the Apocalypse. In this way, Joachim developed the basic divisions of a system of double sevens, thus bringing together *status*, *tempus*, and *etas* into a single parallel. Each epoch had its own sequence of 7, while the overall history of mankind is related to the seven-day week of history.

The chart displays Joachim's overview of history based on the seven-day week of creation. Each epoch contains its own sequences of 7 events unique to that epoch, yet each is parallel to Joachim's overview of 7 major time divisions, which correspond to St. Augustine's seven-day week of historical periods. The major deviation from St. Augustine's is that Joachim places the seventh age in historical time. A reconstruction of all of Joachim's interpretations of the seven seals and the application of those meanings to each age would be too lengthy, but a summary of Joachim's interpretations as they relate to the Second Epoch is crucial because Joachim shows the unity of the Trinity in history by means of those seven seals.[13]

In the *Expositio in Apocalypsim*, part 2,[14] Joachim portrays the opening of the seven seals and the blowing of the seven trumpets as indi-

OLD TESTAMENT		NEW TESTAMENT	
1st seal:	From Abraham or Jacob to Moses and Joshua	1st seal:	From Christ to death of John the Baptist
2nd seal:	Joshua to David	2nd seal:	Death of St. John to Constantine
3rd seal:	David to Elias (Elijah) and Elisha	3rd seal:	Constantine to Justinian
4th seal:	Elisha to Isaiah and Hezekiah	4th seal:	Justinian to Charlemagne
5th seal:	Hezekiah to Judah's Captivity	5th seal:	Charlemagne to the present time (c. A.D. 1200)
6th seal:	Jews return to Malachi's death	6th seal:	Times about to begin
7th seal:	Malachi to John the Baptist and Christ	7th seal:	End of second status, conversion of world, Sabbath

cating that the Christian era allegorically represents significant events in the historical period from Christ to the third age. The seven-seals chronology is outlined to correspond to the seven trumpets blown by the seven angels in Apocalypse 8–11. The concord to this interpretation is found in the Old Testament when the priests appeared before the walls of Jericho, blew their trumpets, and caused them to fall. In the New Testament, the corresponding types are the preachers who raised their voices like trumpets. So as with the walls of Jericho, the contemporary world order would fall, along with the Antichrist, at the final trumpet blast at the end of the sixth *tempus*.

The White Horse that appeared at the opening of the first seal in Apocalypse 6 was envisioned by Joachim as the primitive church dispensing the gospel message while being persecuted by the Jews. The horse's rider is Christ and the "living creature" calling forth the horse is the Apostolic Order announcing the Advent of Christ and inviting the world to contemplation. Correspondingly, the parallel first trumpet represented the Apostles, mainly Paul, proclaiming the gospel message. He interpreted the hail mentioned in this verse as the hardness of Jewish hearts.

The opening of the second seal pictures the emergence of the Red Horse whose rider holds a sword that will disrupt world order through a rampage of killing inflicted on all people. To Joachim, the horse symbolized the Roman pagan priests and armies. The rider was Satan, represented by Roman emperors. In history, this seal loosed the persecution of the early saints and the wars of the later Roman empire. Joachim closed the period with the victory of Constantine over paganism. Just as Joachim saw the Apostolic Order of the first seal as the heralds of Christ, he offset the Red Horse of the second seal with the Order of Martyrs, represented by the second "living creature" roundabout the heavenly throne. The second trumpet blast was the Martyrs and Ante-Nicean Doctors combating the heresy of Nicolaus.

The breaking of the third seal caused the Black Horse to emerge, ridden by a man holding a pair of scales. Joachim saw this as the Arian heresy, whose corrupt clergy is the rider bringing terror and darkness into the Christian faith. The scales (balances) held in the rider's hand refer to the disputed Word (or Arian interpretations), while the wheat, barley, oil, and wine refer to Joachim's historical schema of triads. The "living creature" in this verse represents both the Order of Doctors who proclaimed the truth and the holy men and hermits who instituted the monastic life. The blast of the third trumpet represents the Post-Nicean Doctors who upheld the true faith against these errors. The meteor in this verse is Arius corrupting the Scriptures.

At the opening of the fourth seal, a Pale Horse appears ridden by "Plague" and followed by Hades. This ashen horse is the Saracen, whose rider was Mohammed persecuting Christians. (Joachim also parallels this verse to the little horn of Daniel's fourth beast and to Israel's fourth tribulation at the hands of the Syrians and Assyrians). Order is maintained by the fourth "living creature" that represents the Monks and Virgins who are essential to the stability and survival of the Christian faith. The fourth trumpet Joachim visualized as the Monks and Virgins who furnish light to the world by illuminative contemplation. This light, however, is almost put out by the Moslems.

With the opening of the fifth seal, the writer of the Apocalypse no longer pictures beasts, but envisions the altar of God as the Roman Church come of age. In the first four seals, Christians were persecuted and attacked by external forces that had since passed away. But in the fifth seal, Joachim turns to contemporary events in Spain where the Saracens had killed many Christians over the previous several years. The white robes given to the souls under the altar in this passage signified, Joachim felt, the reward of martyrdom, while the rest of the Scripture indicates that more suffering will occur in church history. The fifth trumpet represents the heretics of Joachim's day, and Joachim here digresses into a lengthy account of heretical sects known to him in the late twelfth century. These heresies are the "scorpion-locusts" of this verse, whereas the "trees and grass" are Christians of simple faith. Joachim believed that Antichrist was already in the world and anticipated that the sixth trumpet blast signified the time when he would become generally known.

The sixth seal opened the Day of Judgment for Babylon, which represented to Joachim any force in opposition to the Church of St. Peter. Joachim here predicts two sequential persecutions of the believers. Especially vulnerable during these tribulations were false Christians and fallen church members in the Holy Roman Empire. The angel blowing the sixth trumpet represented the preachers who announce the loosing of four demons and who cease to pray for Christendom. The four demons are the same that had been bound in Apocalypse 7, still waiting to do evil. These demons represent multiple meanings, and are shown as the external secular enemies of Christendom, infidels, and internal heresies. The sixth *tempus* is a period of extreme tribulation when men turn to worshiping idols and demons. A change occurring at this point is that Joachim becomes much less specific about the events following the opening of the sixth seal, events still in his future. Instead, he discusses types and qualities of events. The chronology of his schema is of extreme importance to Joachim here since the transfer of events from the sixth to the seventh *tempus* coincide, he thought, with the emergence of the Third Epoch. So frightening is the prospect of the tribulations of the sixth *tempus* that Joachim advances to Apocalypse 10 and inserts at this point of his narrative the hope offered by the Angel of Light sent to help the elect to salvation.

Also in this passage, Joachim addresses himself to the "two witnesses" that arise in the midst of these tribulations. Joachim cannot quite make up his mind who these figures are. At first he announces them to be Enoch and Elias, but later he calls them Moses and Elias. Then he decides to approach the whole question figuratively and tells us to expect two spiritual orders, rather than individuals, that come in the spirit of Enoch and Elias to preach and combat the Antichrist.

Before the opening of the seventh seal, St. John, the writer of the Apocalypse, describes the activities of the "Sealing Angel" in Chapter 7. Joachim does not clarify for his readers who this angel is. It could be Christ himself, or a Roman pope specially selected by Christ and through whom he will rebuild his Church. During this time between the opening of the sixth and seventh seals, however, the righteous will triumph, the 144,000 elect will be summoned, and the great battle between the Lamb and the Beast will be fought.

The seventh seal is opened in Verse 1 of Chapter 8 and there is silence in heaven for about half an hour. The "Great Silence," to Joachim, was the last Sabbath of rest in which contemplative silence will bring to reality the words of Psalm 74: "I will be silent to hear what the Lord God may say concerning me." The seventh trumpet represents the revelation of the hidden mysteries of the Scripture. Here will appear great preachers announcing the second coming of Christ. The Beast and false prophet will be cast into Hell, Antichrist and his corrupters will be exterminated, and the Sabbath state, the eighth day of history, will begin.

The New Epoch had been announced by its herald, St. Benedict, and it would be ushered in sometime during the thirteenth century. Joachim never tried to tie God to any exact timetable: ". . . cuius terminus erit in arbitrio Dei."[15]

In the *Liber Concordie*, Joachim first describes how the third epoch would be lived.[16] The defeat of Antichrist at the end of the New Age of the Holy Spirit in which a new spiritual life of peace and contemplation would be the cardinal feature. Under the guidance of the Holy Spirit, a "novus ordo" would become a reality. The question of what sort of earthly institutions would emerge with this new order is still an open question. Certainly Joachim envisioned some sort of Utopia roughly parallel to monasticism in which the various members of Christ's mystical Body, the Church, would achieve great spirituality and harmony of purpose.

In the *Liber Figurarum* appears a diagram of a loosely organized society depending mostly upon a spiritual *entente cordiale* between varying forms of religious life, with the laity under the general direction of a "pater spiritualis" and his monastic associates. This drawing, titled "*Dispositio Novi Ordinis pertinens ad tercium statum*," is composed of a central oratory surrounded by four other oratories with two more attached. The five-two division makes a complete seven-order to represent the third epoch. The total drawing is noticeably in the form of a cross with a predella before it. Property and work are devoted to the community with little notion of personal gain. Social and political advancement is only through spiritual performance as the individual strives to reach the highest level of piety and contemplation in the first oratory. This "New Jerusalem" is meant to picture the ultimate development of life during the third epoch. It does not replace the existing Church, but rather, Joachim believed, was its ultimate evolution.

The state as Joachim envisioned it is well drawn out in the *Liber Figurarum* (Figure III). Basic to his ideal is St. Paul's pronouncement in I Corinthians 12:12 that: "Our bodies have many parts, but the many parts make up only one body when they are all put together. So it is with the body of Christ." The body politic is composed of many members; yet is unified as a living organ. Joachim combined this formula with St. John's vision in Apocalypse 4:1-2 and 6-7, in which the heavenly throne is surrounded by a lion, a calf, a man, and an eagle, and with the statement in Ephesians 4:11-13 that God's gifts to human beings work to the perfection of the body of the Church. The apostles, prophets, evangelists, pastors, and doctors mentioned in Ephesians 4 were commissioned for the work of the pastorate specifically to edify the body of Christ. The end result was to be the unity of the faith, a perfect Christian body politic in the fullness of Christ.

In Figure III we learn immediately that the cluster of five oratories at the top of the drawing are dedicated to contemplatives arranged in four oratories surrounding the fifth, which is inhabited by those men to whom the Holy Spirit has given the gift of counsel. Surrounding these select men of the central oratory are "perfect" students who translate to the hearts of the people what they have learned from these teachers, thus assuring spiritual unity and harmony. In essence, Joachim's spatial drawing shows a formal relationship between monks, secular clergy, and the laity.

Each member of the body of Christ in the last age is represented by a member of the human body—each has a function that relates to the whole, making the whole complete in flesh and spirit. At the center of Joachim's drawing in Figure III is the Oratory of Mary and of the Holy Jerusalem, a house of prayer representing the nose of the body, symbolized by the dove, and functioning as divine counsel to the rest of the body. Joachim labels this oratory as the "Seat of God." The entire community is governed from this oratory by a *pater spiritualis*. He and his associates

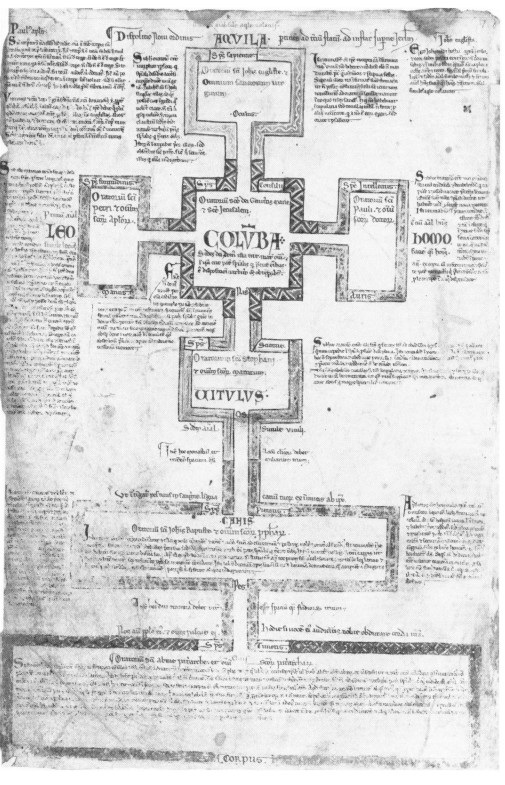

FIGURE III *Dispositio novi ordinis pertinens*   *Bodleian Library, Oxford University*
ad tercium statum ad instar superne Jerusalem

further guide the lives of those in the community by their example and edification. They follow the Cistercian Rule in its purest form.

To the left, and adjacent to the central oratory, is the Oratory of St. Peter and the Holy Apostles. This unit represents the hand; it is symbolized by the lion, and functions as the house for the aged, ill, and handicapped. Joachim calls it the spirit of courage because in spite of multiple infirmities the members of this oratory strive to follow the Rule of the Cistercians in as strict a manner as their health will allow.

Below the central oratory, or counterclockwise, is the Oratory of St. Stephen and the Martyred Saints. This division represents the mouth; it is symbolized by the calf, and it functions as a center of deeper contemplation. The spirit of knowledge is the theme of this house. Herein, brethren are constantly preparing and training themselves for greater spiritual discipline through contemplation and understanding.

To the right of the central oratory is the Oratory of St. Paul and the Doctors of the Church. This house represents the ear; it is symbolized by the man, and it functions as a center of learning. Joachim labels this oratory with the spirit of understanding as this unit houses the scholarly monks of the community.

Above the center oratory is the Oratory of St. John the Evangelist and the Virgin Saints. This unit represents the eye; it is symbolized by the eagle, and its function is total cloistered contemplation. The spirit of wisdom signifies this oratory wherein men and women perfect their lives through continuous prayer and contemplation.

Below the cluster of five oratories, each of which presents the highest ideals of religious life, are two more oratories detached by greater space in the diagram, but still attached. These two house the secular clergy and religious laymen.

Below the Oratory of St. Stephen and the Martyred Saints is the Oratory of St. John the Baptist and the Prophets. This larger house represents the foot; it is symbolized by the dog and its function is to house the secular clergy. Joachim labeled it the spirit of devotion, for its members lived together in renunciation of flesh meat and warm clothing.

At the bottom of the drawing, and at the bottom of the hierarchy, is the Oratory of St. Abraham the Patriarch and all Patriarchs. This division represents the human form; it is symbolized by the sheep, and its function is to house the masses of the married and their children. The spirit here is fear, that is, fear for their salvation. Joachim is more specific in his details at this point. Those in this division will live in private houses, but their lives are to be governed by the *pater spiritualis* and work supervisors. They must be constantly on guard against Satan. All shall work, and lazy persons will be denounced by all and forced by the supervisors to work. Women are assigned domestic duties and are to teach the adolescent girls. All will tithe, and Joachim hints at income leveling and common possession of material goods.

In all his interpretations, Joachim did not consider the end of history but its consummation during the third epoch. In this marvelous time the Church would reach its exaltation through a new form of religious experience and life. The destiny of mankind was a pure religious society in which all would read the Scriptures with "new eyes" that would reveal to them the fullness of God's plan. Just as the Holy Spirit proceeded from both the Father and the Son, so a new understanding of the Gospel message would proceed from the Old Testament and the New, and a new epoch would emerge from the First and Second.

Joachim summarized his vision when he said in the *Liber Concordie* that: ". . . the third [epoch] will be the age of the Holy Spirit, of whom the apostle said: Where there is the spirit of the Lord, there is liberty."[17] According to Joachim's beliefs and interpretations, that day was at hand.

CHAPTER III

Joachim and the Latin Fathers

T HE opening of each of the seven seals marks, according to Joachim of Fiore, the beginning of a new period in the history of the Church. Each of the first six periods is characterized by one of the lesser orders of the elect. The first period of the Church is characterized by the Order of Apostles; the second period, by the Order of Martyrs; the fourth period, by the Order of Monks and Virgins; the fifth period, by the growth of the previous orders in the general Church; the sixth period, by the new orders of laity. The opening of the third seal marks for Joachim the beginning of the third period of the Church, a time in which the Church was defended against the errors of heretics by the Order of Doctors. From among those who forged and championed the doctrines of the Church, Joachim singles out for mention St. Augustine in Africa, St. Jerome in Bethlehem, St. Ambrose in Italy, and Hilary of Poitiers in France.[1] Together with Pope Gregory the Great, who lived during the fourth period in the history of the Church, these men make up the major part of the Latin tradition upon which Joachim draws for his understanding of theology and of history.

St. Augustine is for Joachim the theologian par excellence in the history of the Church. He is the Latin father most frequently quoted by the abbot of Fiore (see Chart of Textual Citations at the end of this chapter). Joachim draws from the bishop of Hippo's *Enchiridion on Faith, Hope and Love*, his sermons on the Gospels, and perhaps his *On the Predestination of the Saints*.[2] The most important works of St. Augustine on which Joachim depends, however, are *De civitate Dei* and *De Trinitate*.

De civitate Dei provides the abbot of Fiore both with historical information and with a method for interpreting that information. Joachim's understanding of the time of the New Testament, for example, is influenced by the analysis of biblical and pagan history done by St. Augustine. In the *Liber Concordie* (9r, 43r), Joachim places the beginning of the

Roman people, called Gentile, with a certain adulterer who begat Romulus and Remus in union with a whore. The abbot of Fiore apparently takes seriously the aspersions cast by St. Augustine on the pagan claim that the twins were born from the union of the god Mars and the Vestal Virgin Rhea (III:3–5; XVIII:21–22).[3] By locating the impetus of the Roman people not with Romulus, founder of Rome, but a generation earlier with his adulterous sire, Joachim accords to the Gentiles a beginning that is parallel to that of the Jews who imitated the corruption of Adam. St. Augustine places the adulterous union that produced Romulus and Remus at the same time when, under the reign of King Uzziah in Judah, prophets began to foretell the coming of Christ into the world (XVIII:27; LC 43r). This information enhances for Joachim the appropriateness of designating the beginning of the time of the New Testament, which flowers in Christ, in Uzziah, the man who claimed the powers of both priest and king.

In the *Expositio in Apocalypsim*, Joachim appeals to St. Augustine's opinions concerning the final events of the world. The abbot frequently cites St. Augustine's statement at the beginning of Book XX that the time occupied by Christ's judgment of the living and the dead is indeterminate, but that all who read the Scriptures know that "day" generally means "time" (EA 81r, 139v, 210r; LC 124v). For Joachim, the nomenclature "time" and designation of an indeterminate length for the "Day of Judgment" means that the events associated with this final judgment unfold within a historical period, or seventh age. In the *Expositio* (140r, 207v), Joachim quotes St. Augustine's designation of the final events (XX:30): Elias (Elijah) will come, the Jews will convert, the Antichrist will unleash a persecution, Christ will descend from heaven for judgment, the good and the evil will be separated, and the world will be consumed by fire and renewed. The Abbot of Fiore also quotes St. Augustine's disclaimer for knowing the precise manner in which these things will be carried out or the sequence in which they will occur. This disclaimer functions in some sense both to warn against exact predictions and to allow Joachim the freedom to modify St. Augustine's sequence. In the figure of "The Seven-Headed Dragon" (Table XIV), for example, Joachim combines the statement of I John 2:18 that there are many Antichrists with the idea gleaned from St. Paul that there is only one (II Thess. 2:3–4). Joachim can then state that the seventh king is properly called the Antichrist and that Gog is the final Antichrist, thus placing a persecution unleashed by the Antichrist and his legions at the beginning and at the end of the seventh age.[4]

More integral to Joachim's theology of history, however, is the method for interpreting this kind of historical data which the abbot also gleans from *De civitate Dei.* Joachim's concordances in the histories of the Old and New Testaments provide the foundation for his various historical schemata. Joachim uses the term *concordia* for his rigorous comparison of person to person, thing to thing, and event to event, and states that the harmony, that is, the *concordia* of the Old and New Testaments, was revealed to him.[5] The patristic roots of this aspect of the abbot's method may perhaps be discerned in *De civitate Dei* in St. Augustine's coordination of the events of biblical and of pagan histories. The bishop of Hippo suggests by this coordination that something is to be learned by placing seemingly disparate events in relation to each other. Occasionally he points out specifically the meaning behind such a relationship, for example, noting that it was appropriate for Rome to be founded at the same time that there arose among the people of Israel the prophets who foretold the coming of Christ. Both Rome and the prophets and their prophecies, St. Augustine asserts, were to be of benefit to all nations (XVIII:27). But whereas St. Augustine places contemporaneous events side by side and allows for some comparison of the qualities and inner structures of the events, Joachim uses *concordia* to compare the people, things, and events of an earlier time with those of a later time. Through this comparison, the abbot sets forth parallel chronologies in history.[6]

Joachim illustrates the symmetry of each parallel chronology by showing a numerical equality in terms of generations. In using generations for his calculations, the abbot is following the lead of Matthew (1:17), whose genealogy of Christ lists fourteen generations from Abraham to David, from David to the Captivity and from the Captivity to Christ. He is also following the lead of St. Augustine, who notes in *De civitate Dei* (XXII:30) that the first two historical periods, Adam to Noah and Noah to Abraham, are equal not in number of years but in number of generations. At the beginning of Book II of the *Liber Concordie* (10v, 13r), Joachim quotes this passage in support of the calculations according to generations with which he is especially concerned in Books II and IV.

Each of Joachim's historical schemata, established through the concordances, reveals an aspect of the divine trinitarian nature. Joachim's understanding of trinitarian doctrine is drawn primarily from St. Augustine's *De Trinitate.* Book I of the *Psalterium decem chordarum,* which is Joachim's most lengthy and systematic discussion of the Trinity, and a

32

section of the *Expositio in Apocalypsim* (31v-38v) devoted to an exposition of the Alpha and Omega and the Tetragrammaton (IEUE) are replete with quotations from *De Trinitate*. Joachim is especially indebted to St. Augustine for his understanding of the qualities and properties that characterize each of the divine Persons and allow them to be distinguished, and for his understanding of the dynamic relationships that hold among the divine Persons and between the Trinity as a whole and creatures. Joachim quotes St. Augustine in regard to the simple nature of the divine substance, and the fact that no matter what combination of divine Persons one addresses, that combination is true God. The abbot also relies on the bishop of Hippo for his understanding of and refutation of the trinitarian heresies of Arianism and Sabellianism.

St. Augustine has importance for Joachim not simply as a great theologian but also as a founder and supporter of the monastic life. Joachim quotes St. Augustine as saying that there are none better than those who make progress in the monasteries (EA 182v, 189v). In the introduction to the *Expositio in Apocalypsim* (19r-v), Joachim interprets each of the six sons of Leah as an order of the religious life. In Reuben is designated the first order of the religious life, instituted by the apostles in the primitive Church. In Simeon is designated the second order, established in Antioch and called simply Christian disciples. In Levi is designated the third order, established in Alexandria and praised by Philo of Judea for the sobriety and conversation of its adherents.[7] In Judah is designated the fourth order, established in Africa by St. Augustine. In Issachar is designated the fifth order, the order of canons regular established in parts of the West by St. Rufus and following the rule that St. Augustine handed down. And finally, in Zebulun is designated the order of Premonstratensians, similar in observance to the canons regular.

Joachim's second major source of inspiration and authority is Pope Gregory the Great. The pope marked, according to Joachim, the twenty-first generation after Christ (LC 45v, 48v). His lifetime fell during the fourth period of the Church, which extended from the Emperor Justinian to Popes Gregory III and Zecharias (LC 40r; EA 130r, 173r). In the *Expositio in Apocalypsim*, Joachim connects two of the signs of the fourth time to the pope. Pope Gregory is the eagle flying in midheaven and calling woe upon the earth (Apoc. 8:13; EA 130r); he is the angel flying in midheaven and calling the earth to fear and worship God (Apoc. 14:6; EA 137r). Joachim shares with his contemporaries an unbounded admiration for the "Doctor Magnus." Of the writings of the erudite pope, the *Dialogues* is of primary importance for Joachim, followed by the *Homilies on Ezekiel* and the *Moralia*, Pope Gregory's commentary on the Book of Job.

The *Dialogues* is composed as a conversation between Pope Gregory the Great and his deacon, Peter. The book is of principal importance within the realm of hagiography, for recounted are incidents in the lives of bishops, popes, deacons, monks and abbots. For Joachim, the *Dialogues* is first and foremost an historical source, providing information about the history of Italy, monastic history, and the lives of kings and ecclesiastical notables. In the *Liber Concordie* (47v-48r), for example, the abbot of Fiore draws from Book IV, Chapter 31 of the *Dialogues* for his information concerning Theodoricus, king of the Goths and enemy of popes and the Catholic faith.

Book II of the *Dialogues* is Joachim's source for the life and miracles of St. Benedict of Nursia. The contribution of Pope Gregory's account to Joachim's understanding and interpretation of St. Benedict's significance is highlighted by the short tract *De vita sancti Benedicti et de officio divino secundum ejus doctrinam* (Concerning the Life of St. Benedict and the Divine Office according to his Teaching). In the first half of this tract, the abbot of Fiore comments on incidents in St. Benedict's life drawn from Book II of the *Dialogues*; in the second half, he comments on selections from the rule that pertain to the nocturnal celebration of the divine office.[8] The intent of Joachim's comments is to place St. Benedict within the schema of salvation history. As did Pope Gregory in the *Dialogues*, Joachim takes care to show that the incidents in the life of St. Benedict are in harmony with the Scriptures. Events in St. Benedict's life find their prototype in biblical events. In harmony with those biblical events, they provide a model of the spiritual life both for the present and for the future.[9]

St. Benedict's importance for Joachim as an eschatological type is predicated on his status as the founder of Western monasticism and the author of the rule par excellence for monastic life. Monastic rules, according to the abbot of Fiore, do not have the authority of the Gospels or writings of the apostles, but they are nonetheless of much use and spiritual value. Commenting on I Kings 18, Joachim states that the four jars of water designate the four volumes of the New Testament which are contained in letters, and he cites the canonical epistles, the Acts of the

Apostles, the Apocalypse, and the rules of the holy fathers. The rules of the fathers are also four in number: the Rule of St. Pachomius, the Rule of St. Basil, the Rule of St. Augustine, and the Rule of St. Benedict (LC 102v). Joachim states that in his rule St. Benedict moderates the stringency of the Greeks, for example, allowing meat to be given to the sick (LC 69r). In *De vita sancti Benedicti* (13:17–25) Joachim notes St. Benedict's mercy and points out that while St. Benedict could lead a rigorous and disciplined contemplative life, he yields to the needs of others, as when he spends the night in discussion and prayer with his sister Scholastica.

On the basis of information gleaned from Pope Gregory's *Dialogues* and his own calculations, Joachim states that St. Benedict was called to the Order of Monks around the end of the sixteenth generation after Christ (LC 11v). The abbot of Fiore places the double beginning of the Order of Monks, which characterizes the third epoch, in the prophet Elisha (first epoch) and in Benedict (second epoch). An association of St. Benedict with both Elisha and Elias is present in the *Dialogues*. Because St. Benedict is a forerunner of the third epoch, he is the Latin father most frequently mentioned in Joachim's writings.

Pope Gregory the Great contributes to Joachim's theology of history, however, more than an account of the life of St. Benedict and other historical details. Pope Gregory's biblical commentaries, especially the *Homilies on Ezekiel* and the *Moralia*, provide Joachim with guides for the interpretation of texts and symbols. In his comments on the pairs of Old Testament saints, for example, Joachim appeals to the authority of Pope Gregory for his interpretation of Ezekiel as a type of Christ (LC 37v). In the same context, Joachim interprets Ephraim to represent the fruits of the Holy Spirit, and cites *Moralia* I:27 in support of the idea that the Holy Spirit enables the mind to conceive and give birth to the seven gifts of the Spirit (LC 28r-v). Perhaps the most important constellation of symbolism that Joachim draws from Pope Gregory is that associated with the wheels (*Rotae*) of Ezekiel 1. In Homily IV on Ezekiel, the pope associates each face of the living creatures (Man, Ox, Lion, Eagle) with one of the Gospels (Matthew, Luke, Mark, John) and with one of the works of Christ (birth, passion, resurrection, ascension). In Homily VI:12, 15, Pope Gregory associates the outer wheel with the Old Testament and the inner wheel with the New Testament. Joachim uses this constellation of symbolism as part of his understanding of the work of Christ and as a principle of organization for his four commentaries (*Liber Concordie, Expositio, Psalterium, Quatuor Evangelia*).[10]

Nor does the abbot of Fiore fail to detect whatever eschatological or apocalyptic elements may be present in Pope Gregory's writings. Commenting on the two witnesses who prophesy for one thousand two hundred and sixty days (Apoc. 11:3; EA 145v-149v), Joachim includes Pope Gregory's opinion that these two witnesses are Enoch and Elias, who will aid in the conversion of the Jews. As both the eagle and the angel who fly in midheaven and proclaim the woes of the earth, Pope Gregory is identified by Joachim as a prophet of the end. The abbot of Fiore asserts that the pope is known to have written many things about the end. Beyond all others, he flew higher through the narrow paths of allegories as if they were the narrow ways of heaven. Joachim declares that Pope Gregory has no equal in proclaiming in his works such calamitous times (EA 130r).[11]

Joachim relies on the biblical commentaries of St. Jerome and St. Ambrose. The association of the wheels of Ezekiel with the Old and New Testaments, and the faces of the living creatures with the Gospels, is present in St. Jerome's commentary on Ezekiel. Nonetheless, Joachim's interpretation of the wheels reflects the fuller symbolism and language found in Pope Gregory's homilies. The abbot of Fiore cites St. Jerome extensively in the *Expositio* with regard to the identity of the two witnesses of Apocalypse 11:3 (EA 145v-149r). In the same context, Joachim appeals to St. Ambrose with regard to the death of Moses (EA 146v-147r).

With regard to trinitarian doctrine, Joachim cites in the *Psalterium decem chordarum* (232r) St. Jerome's Letter XV to Pope Damasus. The abbot of Fiore also knows Hilary of Poitiers' *De Trinitate* and cites it once in the *Psalterium* (233r) and once in the *Quatuor Evangelia* (123:25). Joachim's appeal to these two theologians, however, is minor in comparison with his dependence on St. Augustine's *De Trinitate*.

Although St. Augustine, Pope Gregory the Great, St. Jerome, St. Ambrose, and Hilary of Poitiers are in Joachim's mind the great *doctores* of the Church, their writings are not the only resources upon which Joachim could draw for his theology of history. A great deal of study remains to be done on Joachim's sources and much of this study will be facilitated by the appearance of critical editions of the *Liber Concordie, Expositio in Apocalypsim,* and *Psalterium decem chordarum.* Among the other fathers that Joachim mentions are: St. John Chrysostom (LC 46r, 66v), Origen (EA 75v; TSQE 36:9, 73:5), St. Basil (LC 48r, 69r, 102v),

St. Anthony (PDC 247v; TSQE 189:5), St. Pachomius (LC 102r), Rufus (EA 19v), Boethius (LC 47v), and Haimo of Auxerre (Remigius; EA 210r).[12] Joachim certainly drew much of his historical information from Eusebius' *History of the Church*, although the nature of Joachim's dependence on the bishop of Caesarea remains to be examined. Other sources for historical information which have been suggested are Cassiodorus, Paul the Deacon, and Bede the Venerable.[13] The abbot of Fiore's knowledge of and indebtedness to the standard biblical commentary of the middle ages, the *Glossa ordinaria*, has yet to be carefully examined.

Of Joachim's contemporaries, only St. Bernard of Clairvaux is a certain source. The abbot of Fiore quotes St. Bernard's *De consideratione* with regard to the error of Quaternity (PDC 232r, 234v). That the great Cistercian abbot took care to refute this error may be reflected in Joachim's own concern over this trinitarian heresy. In *De vita sancti Benedicti* and in the *Liber Concordie* (58v-59r), Joachim focuses on St. Bernard's role in the foundation of the Cistercian Order. The abbot of Fiore greatly admires the abbot of Clairvaux and notes that St. Bernard's life, miracles, and knowledge have illumined the Church of his own time. But Joachim may appreciate St. Bernard most as the theologian of his time who combats heresy and calls others to arms (EA 87v).

The theologians contemporary to Joachim to whom he is most often compared are Anselm of Havelberg and Rupert of Deutz.[14] All three men draw upon the doctrine of the Trinity for the purpose of interpreting the events from Creation to Last Judgment. Anselm of Havelberg's account of the history of the Church is set forth in Book I of his *Dialogi*.[15] For the bishop of Havelberg, history is a pedagogical process, the gradual revelation of faith in the Trinity according to the ability of the people to know God. Belief in one God has always characterized the Church, asserts Anselm, but the understanding that this one God is three Persons has come slowly. According to the bishop of Havelberg, the Old Testament clearly reveals God as Father, Creator of the world, but presents the Son only in a veiled manner. The New Testament clearly reveals the Son but only hints at the deity of the Holy Spirit. After Christ ascends, the Holy Spirit is sent to the Church for teaching and completing all truth. Here the divinity of the Holy Spirit is revealed fully and faith in the Trinity is at last proclaimed fully.

Anselm divides the history of the Old Testament into five periods, and considers Christ to have initiated the sixth period in the history of the

Church.[16] Based on the seven seals of Apocalypse 6:1–8:1, Anselm divides this sixth period into seven states (*status*). He considers the Church of his time to mark the fourth state of the sixth period, whereas Joachim considers the Church to mark the sixth time of the sixth age. For both men, however, this stage in the history of the Church is characterized by the emergence of the new religious orders of their day (e.g., canons regular, Premonstratensians, Knights Templar).

Rupert of Deutz's major literary efforts were biblical commentaries. By the end of his life, he had commented on virtually all of the books of the Bible except the New Testament epistles.[17] He entitled his major commentary *De Trinitate et operibus ejus* (Concerning the Trinity and Its Works).[18] Rupert focuses on the individual works of salvation history which by a certain appropriateness may be assigned to a particular Person of the Trinity. According to the abbot of Deutz, the proper work of the Father is creation; the period of history appropriate to the Father extends from the appearance of the first light to the fall of the first human. The proper work of the Son is redemption; the period of history appropriate to the Son and the work of redemption extends from the fall of the first human to the passion of the second one, Jesus Christ, Son of God. The proper work of the Holy Spirit is renewal (*innovatio*); the period of history appropriate to the Spirit and the work of renewal extends from the resurrection of Christ to the general resurrection of the dead at the end of the world.

Both Joachim and Rupert focus on the qualities and works appropriate to each Person of the Trinity, and both seek to demonstrate the equality of the Persons through correspondences most often mediated by number symbolism. For Rupert, for example, the seven days of creation that manifest the work appropriate to the Father correspond to the seven ages of the world that manifest the work of redemption appropriate to the Son. The work appropriate to the Holy Spirit in the renewal of creation is defined primarily by the double resurrection of the dead and corresponds to both the work of the Father and that of the Son. The first resurrection is the resurrection of souls through the remission of sins, which destroys the death in sin that entered with the fall after the first seven days. This work of the Holy Spirit in the resurrection of souls thus corresponds to the work of the Father. The second resurrection is the general resurrection of the bodies of the dead that occurs at the end of time. This resurrection destroys the death of all flesh that occurred through the seven ages of the world. The work of the Holy Spirit in the resurrection of bodies corresponds to the work of the Son in redemption. For Rupert, this set of correspondences demonstrates the equality of the works appropriate to each Person of the Trinity.

All three men remain strongly within the Latin tradition. Their writings may be fruitfully compared with those of other twelfth-century theologians such as Otto of Freising, Gerhoh of Reichersberg, Hildegard of Bingen, Honorius Augustodunensis, Hugh of St. Victor, and Richard of St. Victor. But the abbot of Fiore's contemporaries and near-contemporaries do not hold for him the same authority as the theologians of the past. When Joachim refers to the "orthodox" or "catholic" fathers, he has in mind especially St. Augustine, St. Ambrose, St. Jerome, Hilary, and Pope Gregory the Great.

Textual Citations of the Fathers

by Joachim of Fiore

	Psalterium decem chordarum	Expositio in Apocalypsim	Liber Concordie	Quatuor Evangelia	Other
St. Augustine:	232r	19v	9r	36:14	DAF 11:14–17
	233v	31r	10v	73:9	DAF 13:1–14
	235r	36r	13r	255:17	DAF 34:3–4
	235v	58v	43r		PI 1
	236r	71r	46r		
	240r	81r	61r		
	247v	110v	66v		
	251v	117v	102v		
	261r	118r	124v		
		139v			
		140r			
		182v			
		189v			
		198r			
		207v			
		210r			
		211r			
		214r			

Textual Citations of the Fathers (continued)

	Psalterium decem chordarum	Expositio in Apocalypsim	Liber Concordie	Quatuor Evangelia	Other
Pope Gregory the Great:	242r 247v	44r 48r 85r 102r 130r 146v 148v 173r 181v 198r	11v 28r 28v 37v 45v 47v 48v 49r 79r 84v 98r 100v 101r 108r		DAF 66:11–15 PI 59 VSB
St. Jerome:	232r	19v 71r 110v 117v 133r 146r 146v 148r 148v 198r 214r	46r 66v	15:3 41:1 73:8	
St. Ambrose:		19v 71r 110v 146v 147r	46r 66v	73:8	
Hilary of Poitiers:	233r	71r 110v	46r 66v	123:25	

CHAPTER IV

The Trinity and History

OACHIM OF FIORE'S interest in history is motivated by a concern that is at the same time moral and spiritual. He begins the *Liber Concordie* (Preface) with an exhortation to his contemporaries to prepare for the tribulations which he thinks are soon to come. They must awaken from their moral turpitude and arm themselves with the weapons of the spirit. They must entrust themselves to Christ so that when the final events begin to press upon them, they will not be caught in revelry and feasting but will be leading a way of life acceptable to God. The preparation Joachim envisions involves knowing the final events of the world, for example, the coming of pseudoprophets who would unleash persecutions against the Church. But for the abbot of Fiore, one can know these events only by knowing the whole course of revealed history, past and future. Only by examining the whole drama of events from Creation to Last Judgment can that symmetry be perceived, that is, the ordering of salvation history. The resulting vision of the past and future gives the sense of immediacy and urgency, which is part of Joachim's apocalypticism and which is communicated clearly in his calling of his contemporaries to moral reform. But this vision of past and future also communicates the spiritual dimension of history, for it is a vision of the working of God. Joachim considers that God has ordered history so as to reveal the divine trinitarian nature, and so through history one can come to know and to contemplate the Trinity in all its dynamic relationships.

Joachim's commentaries offer as it were a spirituality based on the historical content of Scripture. For the abbot the events and *dramatis personae* of sacred history must be carefully studied, for the details and sequences which are manifested on the literal-historical level of Scripture are images of divine reality on the spiritual level. In the study of Scripture Joachim's concern is always to move from the literal-historical understanding to the spiritual understanding. His approach to Scripture is christocentric, drawn especially from the letters of St. Paul, and his method of interpretation involves the principle of *concordia* and the twelve so-called spiritual principles, five allegorical and seven typological. Joachim's method of interpretation contributed significantly to his understanding of salvation history as an image of that doctrine of the Trinity that had been handed down by the fathers.

The abbot of Fiore is quite clear that Christ is the sole revealer of the mysteries and secrets of the Bible.[1] By secrets (*secreta*) and mysteries (*mysteria*) he means expressions of the divine purpose in human history which are not yet fully revealed.[2] For Joachim, Christ accomplished a definitive revelation of the divine mysteries through His Resurrection. In this context, he speaks about Christ only in an active sense as the revealer, never about Christ as the one who is revealed. By overcoming death and rising triumphant from the tomb, Christ as the Lion from the Tribe of Judah was found worthy to open the book sealed with the seven seals (Apoc. 5:1–5). Joachim states that in the opening of this book Christ makes known the meaning of all things. By "all things" Joachim means generally the persons and events of human history. Thus, the abbot sees this revelation as complete. But he is also clear that people are not able to comprehend the whole revelation at one time and that concessions had to be made to human capabilities. Christ, who contains the treasure of teaching (*Thesaurus doctrine*) in his bosom, is in essence the administrator of revelation. Joachim states that Christ himself made concessions to human understanding, giving a full knowledge of some things and leaving other things still hidden. Those things that are still partially hidden are the events of the end times, the tribulations, pseudoprophets, terrors, and hardships. One cannot discover the meaning of these still hidden mysteries alone but must entrust oneself to Christ. Joachim observes that Christ reveals his secrets only to those whom he has chosen (*electi*). This means that the whole self must be given over to Christ, the end of all perfection.[3]

The abbot of Fiore uses strictly Pauline language to draw distinctions regarding one's ability to understand the Scriptures and thus to penetrate the mysteries of God.[4] He first draws upon St. Paul's differentiation between natural men (*viri animales*) and those spiritual men (*viri spirituales*) who are conformed to Christ (I Cor. 2:14–15). According to St. Paul, there were mysteries that could be made known only to spiritual men, that natural men could not perceive. For Joachim natural men, in a general sense, include all those people who still cling to the world and thus to "the old man of dust" (I Cor. 15:48). In a more specific sense, they are the Jews who, having rejected Christ, still remain in darkness. Being involved in worldly affairs, they can know only worldly things and cannot penetrate beyond the "letter" of Scripture. To move to an understanding of spiritual realities, one must put off the old man of dust and put on Christ and become a spiritual man. One must, through baptism, have died with Christ to the flesh, to the law, and to the letter, and have been reborn with Christ in the spirit. Thus, for Joachim, one's entire person must be made in Christ's likeness and one must begin to imitate Christ, the heavenly man (I Cor. 14:48–49). Consequently, the abbot's admonition to his Christian contemporaries is to clean their minds and eyes from dust, to leave behind earthly things, and to move to a knowledge of heavenly matters (LC, Preface, 5r).

Joachim bases his plan for the study of Scripture on St. Paul's explanation in I Cor. 14:46 that "the natural precedes the spiritual," and his comment in I Cor. 13:9–12 that when he was a child he thought, spoke, and reasoned like a child, but when he was a man he gave up childish ways. Joachim considers that even those who have taken on the image of Christ, that is, spiritual men, must begin their learning on a basic level and ascend higher. For the abbot, the basic or child's level of understanding Scripture pertains to the letter. Understanding the Bible according to the letter (*secundum litteram*) involves a thorough knowledge of the history contained in the two Testaments, their similarities and differences. This knowledge is gained by using the principle of harmony (*concordia*) of the Old and New Testaments.

The abbot defines harmony as a "likeness of equal proportion between the Old and New Testaments based on number rather than worth" (LC 8r).[5] The twelve patriarchs of the Old Testament, for example, correspond to the twelve apostles of the New Testament; the seven battles of the Jews, to the seven battles of the Church. In working out the correspondences between the two Testaments, Joachim includes the history of the Church up to the Last Judgment under the rubric "New Testament." These numerical correspondences show the harmony, that is, the continuity of the history contained in the two Testaments and later history of the Church. By showing the repeated numerical patterns, these correspondences also indicate the ways in which history may be divided into periods. Joachim considers this literal knowledge of sacred history with its harmonies the "milk of Scripture" (see I Cor. 3:1–3). Once one has considered thoroughly these harmonies from a number of viewpoints, one can and indeed must move on to the adult, spiritual understanding of Scripture.

For Joachim, understanding Scripture according to the spirit (*secundum spiritum*) means moving from the historical into matters of faith. Being thoroughly familiar with sacred history, one can begin with a particular biblical person or event and discern a theological meaning therein. Here the abbot of Fiore uses twelve "spiritual" principles, which he divides into two groups: five principles of the allegorical understanding (*allegoricus intellectus*) and seven principles of the typological understanding (*typica intelligentia*). Joachim discusses his method of exegesis according to the spirit in the *Liber Concordie*, Book V (60v-61v), at the conclusion of his introduction to the *Expositio in Apocalypsim* (26r-v), and in the *Psalterium decem chordarum* (264r-266r).

Joachim notes that the five allegorical principles are general ways of understanding the Bible and that they may be distinguished by proper names. He defines allegory in a general sense as the "likeness of a small thing to a very great one" (LC 8r). Abraham, for example, can designate the Order of Married according to one understanding, or God the Father according to another. Each of the five principles is a species of allegorical understanding that relates "a small thing to a very great one." The historical understanding (*historia intelligentia*) relates a person to a person regarding a quality of worth. According to this understanding, Sarah, for example, represents a free woman, while Hagar represents a slave. Joachim realizes that this understanding differs little from the principle of harmony. But the historical understanding can be used as moral exhortation ("you be like Sarah"), whereas the principle of harmony deals only with the numerical correspondences between historical things. The moral understanding (*moralis intelligentia*) is the likeness of a visible thing to an invisible one: for example, Hagar represents the servitude of the flesh; Sarah represents spiritual leisure. The tropological understanding (*tropologica intelligentia*) relates to doctrine: Hagar signifies the letter; Sarah, the spiritual understanding the words of God. The contemplative understanding (*contemplativa intelligentia*) teaches one to leave behind the flesh and cross to the spirit: Hagar thus signifies the active life; Sarah, the contemplative life. Finally, the anagogical understanding (*anagogica intelligentia*) teaches one to despise earthly things and to love heavenly things: Hagar signifies the present life; Sarah, the future life. Joachim notes that these five allegorical principles represent in an appropriate way the mystery of the Trinity. Each relates to one of five possible relationships involving the divine Persons: the relation of the Father to the Son, the relation of the Son to the Father, the relation of the Father and Son to the Holy Spirit, the relation of the Son and Holy Spirit to the Father, and the relation of all three to creatures (LC 61v). When commenting allegorically, Joachim does not give every passage an interpretation based on each of the five senses, nor does he always state which of the five principles he is using. Rather, he is content to state simply what a person or event "signifies" or "designates" and only occasionally notes when he is using a particular sense.

According to the seven species of the typological understanding, the persons of salvation history are types of the Church. Joachim does not differentiate the seven species by definition or name but only by example. In the *Liber Concordie* the abbot uses Hagar and Sarah as examples; in the *Psalterium* he adds Abraham. Joachim also connects each understanding to one of seven possible ways of confessing the Trinity that witness to the divine unity. Citing an argument of St. Augustine against the Arians, Joachim observes that whether one calls upon one Person of the Trinity, two Persons, or all three, God still responds. According to the first typological understanding, which is appropriate to the Father, Abraham represents the priests of the Jews; Hagar, the Israelite people; Sarah, the tribe of Levi, which was to live from the work of the people. According to the second typological understanding, which is appropriate to the Son, Abraham represents the bishops; Hagar, the church of the laity; Sarah, the church of the clerics. According to the third typological understanding, which is appropriate to the Holy Spirit, Abraham represents the priests serving monasteries; Hagar represents the church of lay people living under monastic rule (*conversi*); and Sarah, the church of monks. According to the seventh typological understanding, which pertains to all three Persons of the Trinity, Hagar represents the churches of the first and second epochs (*status*) which lead the active life; Sarah represents the church of contemplation, peace, and rest of the seventh age (*etas*). Joachim notes that these are the four typological understandings that are generally used and that he himself uses in his commentary on the creation story of Genesis 1 in the *Liber Concordie* (61v-73v). The first typological understanding deals with the first epoch; the second, with the second epoch; the third, with the third epoch; the fourth, with the seven ages of the world.

Joachim states that the fourth, fifth, and sixth typological understandings are not commonly used, and he passes over them quickly. According to the fourth typological understanding, which pertains to the Father and the Son, Abraham signifies the bishops of the Jews and Greeks; Hagar signifies the synagogue; and Sarah, the church of the Greeks. According to the fifth typological understanding, which pertains to the Father and Holy Spirit, Abraham signifies the priests of the Jews and the bishops of the Latin people; Hagar, the synagogue (as in the fourth understanding); Sarah, the church of the Latin people. In the sixth typological understanding, which pertains to the Son and Holy Spirit, Abraham signifies the priests of the second and third epochs; Hagar, the church of workers (those leading the active life); Sarah, the spiritual church of quiet and contemplation. At the conclusion of his commentary on Genesis 1, Joachim notes briefly three different ways the seven ages (*etates*) may be divided according to these three typological understandings. In summary, the abbot states that in all seven typological understandings, Abraham represents the prelates of the church from the beginning until the end of the world; Hagar, the church of the elect who lead an active life; Sarah, the spiritual church, the church of contemplation.[6]

Joachim carefully planned his three major commentaries, the *Liber Concordie*, *Expositio in Apocalypsim*, and *Psalterium decem chordarum*, as well as the unfinished *Tractatus super Quatuor Evangelia*, according to this approach to the study of Scripture, moving from an understanding according to the letter to an understanding according to the spirit, from the harmony of the two Testaments to the twelve spiritual principles. On one level, Joachim's four commentaries are organized on the basis of the specific scriptural materials. On another level, however, they are organized so as to reflect certain biblical images, principally the wheel within a wheel of Ezekiel 1 with its four living creatures. The abbot uses these images to relate the four commentaries to each other in one grand design (see outlines following this chapter).

Books I–IV of the *Liber Concordie* are Joachim's study of biblical and ecclesiastical history as well as the various ways history can be divided. In Book I the abbot prepares for his discussion of the harmonies with a brief review of the judgments of God against the sons of Israel and their seven conflicts with foreign nations. His clearly stated purpose is to provide a firm foundation in Old Testament history so that the parallels with church history may be easily seen (LC 3v). Books II and III of the *Liber Concordie* are Joachim's discussion of the special harmonies of the Old and New Testaments. The subject matter of these special harmonies consists of genealogical lists (Book II, Tract I), genealogical trees (Book II, Tract II), and the seven seals of the Old Testament and their openings in the New Testament (Book III). Joachim notes that these harmonies are special because they are calculated by number groups of sevens and tens (LC 13r, 25r-v, 42r). He limits his use of allegory here to showing that the saints of salvation history (1) bear the type of the Trinity, and (2) bear the type of the three social orders (Order of Married/Laity,[7] Order of Clerics, Order of Monks). These two uses of allegory are necessary first to establish the appropriateness of the persons whom Joachim chooses to begin each series of generations, and second to show the significance of each generation list, tree, and seal as itself the bearer of a higher mystery.

Noting that he has surveyed Old Testament history as a foundation for his work and has commented on the special places of harmony under the limits of the numbers seven and ten (LC 42r), Joachim takes up in Book IV the general harmony between the Old and New Testaments. This general, full harmony is not limited by number nor does Joachim use it as a basis for illustrating the relation of the three epochs, three orders, and three divine Persons. In the first two sections (42r-56v) Joachim simply makes a generation-by-generation comparison of Israelite and church history, taking up the popes where the New Testament "generations" cease. His emphasis in interpretation again is on the theological significance of the parallels between the two histories. In the third section (56v-60r) Joachim summarizes his preceding discussions in terms of the three epochs.

Joachim's purpose in these first four books is to indicate the unity of human history, whether that history is divided into two "Testaments" or three epochs, and whether each manner of division is characterized respectively by two peoples (Jews/Gentiles) or by three orders (Married/Clerics/Monks). Based on numerical correspondences, Joachim's method of harmony defines temporally the periods of history and their characteristic peoples or orders, shows their parallels, and thus indicates their unity and equality. As Joachim interprets the harmonies, his comments tend to focus on the theological parallels (e.g., sons born according to the flesh in the Old Testament, sons adopted according to the spirit in the New). Nonetheless, Joachim is careful to remind the reader of the limits of his method of harmony. He states firmly that while there are literal parallels between the two Testaments, for example, there are also spiritual differences. The difference between the Old Testament and the New Testament is the difference between earth and heaven, between moon and sun (LC 5v-6r, 12r, 42r-43v). The Old Testament refers to the flesh; the New Testament, to the spirit. Thus, while the method of harmony establishes the literal parallel, the reader must keep in mind that one part of the harmony (Old Testament) refers to something carnal, while the other part (New Testament) refers to something spiritual.

Joachim's discussion of history through the literal parallels between the two Testaments is the necessary preparation and foundation for understanding fully the spiritual differences between the two peoples and their respective Testaments, and the differences among the three orders and their respective epochs. At the beginning of Book V of the *Liber Concordie*, which is Joachim's interpretation according to the spirit, he summarizes his efforts in these first four books:

> We have arranged the four books of harmonies thus far so as to correspond to the number and likeness of the four animals. Thus the first book, in which the histories are simply compiled, is referred to the man. The second, in which it is a matter of the special and more evident places of harmonies, is referred to the ox. The third, in which it is a matter of the harmonies of the seven seals, is referred to the lion. The fourth, in which it is a matter of the fullness of harmony, is referred to the eagle. Indeed in these four books it is less a matter according to the spirit than according to the letter, that is, according to the harmony of the letter, the letter namely of the two Testaments. But only after the four great works of Christ, in which he was born, suffered, rose, and ascended into heaven (and through which he conforms to the four animals) is the divine shown in the fifth order of fire. Thus the spiritual understandings proceed from these historical words. (LC 60v)

This succinct statement gives firm evidence of the many-leveled order that Joachim gives to his works as a whole and to each commentary individually. Each of the four books of the *Liber Concordie*, marking a progression from simple to more difficult material, is symbolized by one of the four faces of the living creatures in Ezekiel's wheel, and through the living creatures by one of the four great works of Christ. The four books themselves thus prepare for Book V, the book of the spiritual understandings, symbolized by the fifth order of fire.

Book V of the *Liber Concordie* together with the *Expositio in Apocalypsim*, *Tractatus super Quatuor Evangelia*, and *Psalterium decem chordarum* are Joachim's allegorical commentaries, his interpretation according to the spiritual understanding. The abbot expresses the interrelationship of his allegorical commentaries on the historical books of the Bible in terms of Ezekiel's vision of the wheel within a wheel (LC 112v-113v; EA 2v-3r). According to Joachim (see Figure IV), the outer wheel is the general history of the Israelite people from Adam to Ezra and Nehemiah. Although written in segments by various authors, the narratives were finally gathered together and assembled in the Old Testament in a continuous history of the sons of Israel. The inner wheel is the general history of the Church as it is expressed in the Apocalypse. The Apocalypse contains the key to understanding the future events of the Church, not only in history but also after the end of the world. Through understanding those events, one can also discern the previously hidden meaning of past history. Thus the general history of the Apocalypse corresponds to the general history in the Old Testament.

Joachim considers the *Liber Concordie*, Book V, Parts I–III, his commentary on the general history of the Old Testament according to the spiritual understanding. In Part I, the abbot uses the seven species of the typological understanding to comment on the seven days of Creation. In Part II, he comments on the Book of Genesis, beginning with the Flood, and very briefly on Exodus. In Part III, he comments on the four Books of Kings, with references to Chronicles and Ezra. He does not comment on Joshua, Judges, or Ruth. This allegorical commentary on the general history of the Old Testament corresponds to his allegorical commentary on the general history of the Church, that is, the *Expositio in Apocalypsim*.

Joachim states that within each of the two general histories are four special histories. These four spiritual histories are symbolized in the four faces of each living creature within the wheel in Ezekiel's vision. According to Joachim, the four special histories of the Old Testament are Job, Tobit, Esther, and Judith. Joachim argues that these histories are distinguished from others by a certain spiritual grace. They contain things of universal concern and speak about various mysteries. The four Gospels are the four spiritual histories within the general history of the Church.

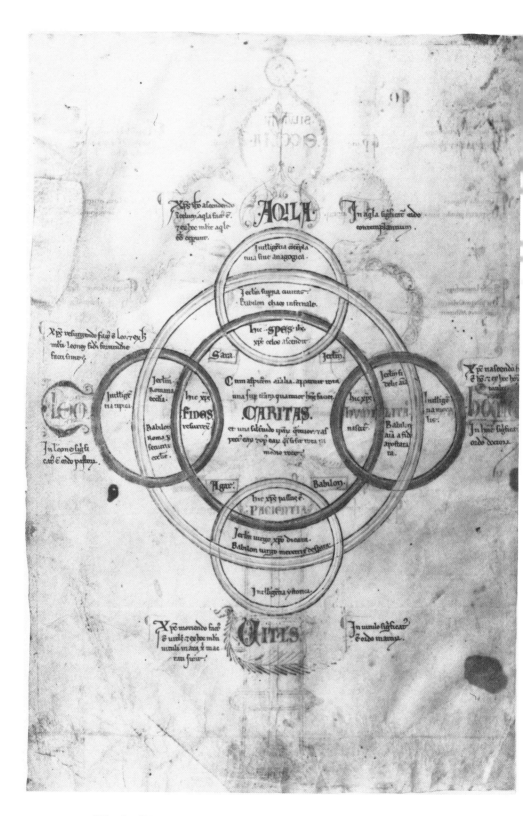

FIGURE IV Wheels of Ezekiel

Joachim relates each of the Old Testament histories to one of the four Gospels through four of the great works of Christ. Both Job and Matthew relate to the Nativity of Christ. Tobit and Luke relate to the Passion of Christ. Judith and Mark relate to Christ's Resurrection, and Esther and John relate to his Ascension. The abbot notes moreover that the Jews do not accord Tobit and Judith canonical authority, although the Church does. This lack of canonical authority is appropriate, for their New Testament corollaries, Mark and Luke, were disciples of apostles and only describe what they have heard rather than what they have seen. Thus, the outer wheel, the general history of the Old Testament, has its four faces in Job, Tobit, Judith, and Esther; the inner wheel, the general history contained in the Apocalypse, has its four faces in Matthew, Luke, Mark, and John (VSB 22:35-69; LC 113v; EA 3r). Book V, Part IV, of the *Liber Concordie* is Joachim's commentary on Job, Tobit, Judith, and Esther.

Joachim ends the *Liber Concordie* with a commentary on the minor prophets (Book V, Part V) and on the major prophets (Book V, Part VI) in order to show that what he has previously said has been in line with the authority of these men (LC 122v). The *Liber Concordie* is the most intricately organized of Joachim's commentaries, beginning with the four books of harmonies and ending with an allegorical commentary on most of the historical and all of the prophetic books of the Old Testament. The images that Joachim uses to relate the parts of this commentary to each other he also uses to relate the commentary to the *Expositio* and *Tractatus*.

The commentary that is not included specifically under the rubric of the wheel within a wheel and the living creatures is the *Psalterium decem chordarum*. Yet this commentary is perhaps the culmination of Joachim's exegetical efforts. More than the *Liber Concordie, Expositio,* and *Tractatus,* the *Psalterium decem chordarum* shows that Joachim's theology of history relates to his experience of the liturgy as prescribed by the Benedictine Rule. Especially important for Joachim is the prescription that all hundred and fifty Psalms should be chanted every week (Rule XVIII; PDC 277v). The abbot considers this chanting of the psalms in praise of God to be the primary vocation of the Order of Monks (PDC 244r, 245r, 277v). This chanting, moreover, was the focal point of his contemplation of the Trinity. Joachim reports that his clearest insight into the doctrine of the Trinity came one Pentecost while chanting the psalms, when the figure of the Psaltery of Ten Strings was revealed to him (PDC 227r-v). The

Psalterium grows out of this experience, and the abbot dedicates it to the glory and praise of the Trinity.

The *Psalterium decem chordarum* is not a verse-by-verse commentary on the Psalms. Joachim divides his work into three books. At the basis of Joachim's exposition in Book I is the figure of the Psaltery of Ten Strings. He considers it appropriate to dedicate this Book, "On the Contemplation of the Trinity," to the Father, "by whom are all things." Divided into seven parts, Book I is Joachim's most systematic discussion of the doctrine of the Trinity. Joachim ascribes Book II, "On the Number of the Psalms," to the Son, the Divine Wisdom "through whom are all things." Here Joachim contemplates the perfection of the works of the Trinity. Using numbers (e.g., three, five, seven, ten, twelve, fifteen, twenty, thirty, one hundred and fifty), he shows how the three orders of the elect (244v-257r), the twelve principles of the spiritual understanding (263v-271v), and the generations of the world (271v-277v) reflect the perfection of the works of the Trinity. Joachim dedicates Book III, "On the Institution of Chanting the Psalms," to the Holy Spirit, "in whom are all things." In this brief book it is evident that Joachim's intention to persuade his contemporaries to contemplate the Trinity has in some sense been fulfilled. Here there are no exhortations to leave the world but only the conviction that praise of God is a matter for all Christians. Nonetheless, the monks are especially called to such praise, as is evident in their liturgy. Joachim closes the *Psalterium* by noting that the very arrangement of the decades of the psalms in the Benedictine Rule reflects the perfection of the Trinity.

The symmetry of history that is established by the principle of harmony and interpreted by the twelve spiritual principles reflects for Joachim the perfect symmetry of the Trinity. But for the abbot of Fiore the self-revelation of God in history is more complex than might be indicated by the assertion that the Three are One and the One is Three. All possible relations among the divine Persons, and between the Trinity as a whole and creatures, have been made part of the divine ordering of events. As noted, Joachim's commentaries are devoted to making clear the trinitarian nature of history, but the abbot has reserved his most systematic and theoretical discussion of the doctrine of the Trinity for Book I of the *Psalterium decem chordarum*. In setting forth his understanding of the Trinity, Joachim draws inspiration from two sources. The first is the tradition of those fathers who have defended the faith against heresy, the *patres catholici et orthodoxi* (PDC 229r, 234v, 236r). He relies heavily on St.

Augustine's *De Trinitate*, following the bishop of Hippo *ad sensum* and frequently quoting directly (PDC 230r, 233v, 235v, 235r).[8] He draws some additional support from Hilary of Poitiers' *De Trinitate* (PDC 233r), St. Jerome's Letter XV to Pope Damasus (PDC 232r), and St. Bernard of Clairvaux's *De consideratione* (PDC 232r, 234v). In addition to this appeal to tradition, Joachim uses a second kind of evidence, based on his conviction that the world mirrors divine reality. He illustrates the subtle thoughts of the fathers with concrete analogies drawn both from Scripture and from nature. The predominant metaphor used by Joachim to illustrate the doctrine of the Trinity is the triangular-shaped, ten-stringed Psaltery, an instrument of "beautiful form, gracious sound, and sweet modulation" (PDC 228v).

According to Joachim, the orthodox confession of the doctrine of the Trinity is that God is one God without confusion of Persons and three Persons without division of substance. The abbot understands the unity of the Trinity to reside in the divine substance which is simple (*simplex*) in nature. He predicates the life, equality, co-eternal majesty, and sharing of properties and characteristics among the three Persons to the divine substance. God cannot change, be divided, suffer, decrease, or increase. God always was, is, and shall be that which He is. Yet the distinction between the three Persons based on their "origin" is also a part of this simple divine nature. God the Father is unbegotten (*ingenitus, a nullo*), the Son is begotten by the Father (*genitus, natus*), and the Holy Spirit proceeds from both (*ab utroque procedens*). Joachim is clear that this divine activity is eternal, and he appears to have been fascinated by the idea that there would be such movement within the deity without sundering the one substance. Indeed, his explanation of the Trinity and the trinitarian nature of history is a commentary as it were on the dynamism represented by the attributes unbegotten, begotten, and proceeding.

Closely associated with the distinguishing of the Persons as unbegotten, begotten, and proceeding are the relationships which hold among the three Persons. With St. Augustine, Joachim explains that the three Persons are named in relation to each other. The Father, the Unbegotten, is so named because he has a Son; the Son, the Only Begotten, is so named because he has a Father; and the Holy Spirit is named in relation to the Father and the Son because he proceeds from both. Joachim also enumerates five possible relationships involving the divine Persons: (1) the relation of the Father to the Son, since the Father is one father of one son; (2) the relation of the Son to the Father, as the Son is one son of one father; (3) the relation of the Father and Son to the Holy Spirit, since both send the Spirit; (4) the relation of the Son and Spirit to the Father, since both are sent by the Father; (5) the relation of all three to each creature, since these three Persons are one God and one Creator.[9] And because the three Persons are one God, Joachim states that there are seven possible ways of confessing the Trinity. For whether one calls upon one Person of the Trinity, two Persons, or all three, God still responds.

Joachim thus affirms the ineffable unity of the Trinity and holds that whatever is said according to substance is said equally of the Father, Son, and Spirit. The Persons of the Trinity, for example, may each be called a beginning. The Father is the beginning of the Holy Spirit because the Spirit proceeds from both and is given by both to humanity. The Holy Spirit is called a beginning, since by His inspiration He is the beginning of all good works; as God, the Spirit is the beginning of all creatures. Yet these are not several beginnings but only one beginning. Joachim also applies this reasoning to works such as the Incarnation and sending of the Holy Spirit, and to qualities such as wisdom, love, and goodness. These works and qualities are shared by the three Persons through the unity of the divine substance and are without comparative merit or quantity.

But Joachim also holds that while works and qualities are shared equally by the three Persons because of their unity, nonetheless these works and qualities are also the properties that characterize one or another of the divine Persons. To express the idea of properties that subsist in the divine unity but belong especially to one divine Person, Joachim uses the terms *proprium*, *proprietas*, and *proprie*. He applies the term *proprium* generally to those characteristics whose designation is not transferred from one Person to another. For example, it is the property (*proprium*) of the Father to be a father, that of the Son to be a son, and that of the Spirit to be a spirit (PDC 234v). Temporality is a property of the Son and of the Holy Spirit as these Persons are sent into the world, the Son in human flesh, the Spirit in the forms of a dove and tongues of fire. Yet Joachim is quite clear that the properties of paternity, sonship, and spiration do not sunder the divine unity and that the works of the Incarnation and of the sending of the Holy Spirit are works of the whole Trinity (PDC 239r-240r).

Joachim uses the term *proprietas* and the formulas "by its very nature pertains to" (*pertinet proprie*) and "by its very nature is ascribed to" (*ascribitur proprie*) to relate qualities and works to specific Persons of the Trinity. Wisdom, for example, is a special characteristic (*proprietas*) of the Son. Fear is a quality which by its very nature pertains (*pertinet proprie*) to the Father. The Order of Monks by its very nature is ascribed (*ascribitur proprie*) to the Holy Spirit. The abbot uses these terms to indicate that the qualities and works which may thus be ascribed to one divine Person do not exclude the other Persons.

Maintaining the unity of the Trinity is of such importance for Joachim that he takes care to refute three heresies which he thinks threaten the substance of the Trinity. A mistake of heretics, he asserts, is that they do not understand that one can only contemplate heavenly things through lesser, humbler ones. At the beginning of the *Psalterium* (229r) Joachim has recourse to an analogy to trees to define these three erroneous formulations of the doctrine of the Trinity. The image of a tree is a favorite of Joachim for illustrating his theories. He is perhaps also inspired here by St. Augustine's use of that image, as well as several others, to illustrate proper and improper ways of defining the three Persons (*De Trinitate* VII:4). The first error is that the divine substance may be divided into three, as the olive, myrtle, and palm are all trees but are of three different natures. This is the error held by the Arians, who define the attributes of God according to substance, thus confessing the Trinity to be three Persons, each distinct in essence and majesty. The second error would liken the Trinity to three olive trees, the same in nature but having three distinct bodies. The Sabellians hold this error, stating that God is one (*unus*) and is Father, Son and Holy Spirit by his own wish (*pro velle suo*). The third error would liken the Trinity to one tree, of which the root is the divine substance and the branches are the three Persons. This error introduces a quaternity rather than a Trinity, making the divine substance a "fourth something" (*quartum aliquid*) separable from the three Persons. Joachim apparently thought this was the error of Peter Lombard's formulation of trinitarian doctrine.[10]

Against the errors of the Arians and Sabellians, Joachim uses three arguments. First, Joachim affirms that the divine substance is one, simple in nature. Against the Arians, he states that the qualities of "unbegotten," "begotten" and "proceeding" do not indicate a difference in substance. And, as noted above, the names of the Persons are given in relation to each other. Against the Sabellians, who state that the three Persons are one (*tres personae sunt unus*), Joachim holds that the correct confession is that the Father, Son, and Spirit are one God (*pater, filius, et spiritus sanctus sunt unus deus*) and that the three Persons are one (*tres personae sunt unum*).

Second, against both the Arians and Sabellians, Joachim asserts that the names of the Trinity are not empty names but denote three complete, co-eternal and co-equal Persons. With St. Augustine, Joachim affirms the ineffable unity of the Trinity, so that whatever is said according to substance is said equally of Father, Son, and Spirit. Third, the abbot states that while works and qualities are said equally of the three Persons because of their unity, nonetheless these works may by their very nature be assigned to one Person.

In refutation of the error of quaternity, Joachim states that the divine nature of God is God's essence, and by essence is meant substance. According to Joachim, both the three Persons and the divine essence are spoken of according to substance. The term "person" is given in the plural to indicate a plurality and to avoid the notion of singularity, while the term "substance" retains unity and admits no division.[11] The three Persons are said to be one substance in the same manner that the tribes of Judah, Benjamin, and Levi are called one people. As the designation "one people" is not a "fourth something" but the unity of the tribes, so the divine essence is not a "fourth something." (PDC 232r-v).

It is the symbol of the Psaltery of Ten Strings which for Joachim is the symbol par excellence of the orthodox doctrine of the Trinity, maintaining the unity of the three Persons while at the same time expressing the dynamic relationship among them. The figure of the Psaltery from the *Liber Figurarum* (see Figure V) illustrates the way in which Joachim conceived of the instrument as an image of the Trinity.[12] The instrument itself represents the unity of the Trinity in the divine substance. The Psaltery cannot be divided into parts without ceasing to be the musical instrument that it is, yet it consists of three corners. For Joachim the blunted top of the Psaltery represents the Father, while the sharp left corner represents the Son, and the sharp right corner represents the Holy Spirit. This one instrument thus has three corners and the three corners produce the one instrument. The equality of the three Persons, particularly with regard to qualities and works, is also represented in the Psaltery. Despite the blunted top, the Psaltery possesses in Joachim's mind the shape of an equilateral triangle. He asserts that one corner contains as much as the three corners at the same time and that no one corner con-

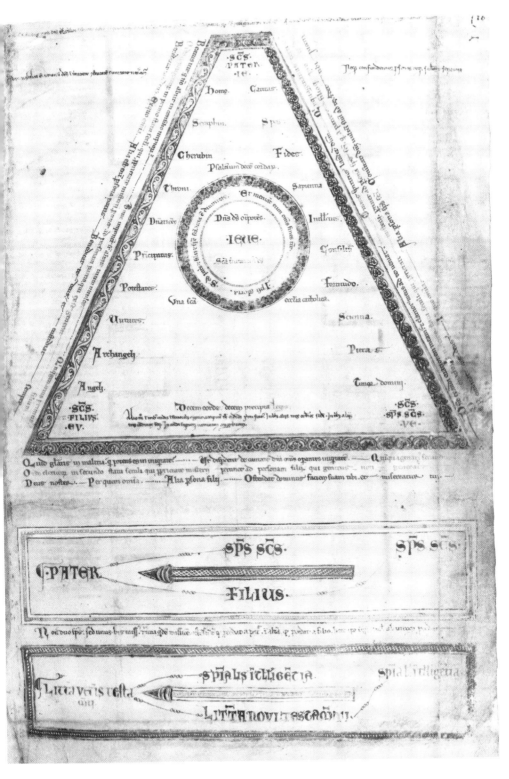

FIGURE V *Psalterium decum chordarum*   Bodleian Library, Oxford University

tains more or less than any of the others. Thus the Father, Son, and Spirit possess equally, without quantity or merit, those qualities which by their very nature may be assigned to only one Person.

The doctrine of the Trinity pervades all of Joachim's thought about history. He is concerned about a correct understanding of the three Persons and one substance, for this is the key to a knowledge of history and of the Trinity itself. Not only individual persons and events but also the whole of history has been ordered to bear the type of the Trinity. For Joachim the historical divisions are related to the doctrine of the Trinity in a way that goes far beyond the popular nomenclature of an "Age of the Father, Age of the Son, Age of the Holy Spirit." Joachim's divisions of history and the orders and works that characterize each temporal period clearly show his conviction of the unity of the Trinity as well as the co-equality and majesty of the three Persons. The times (*tempora*) of the two Testaments, the three epochs (*status*), and the seven ages (*etates*) are Joachim's basic historical divisions, each of which reveals an aspect of the Trinity. For the abbot of Fiore the relationship between the times of the two Testaments and the three epochs manifests the inner dynamism which holds among the three Persons. The schema of the seven ages, on the other hand, indicates the unity of history and thus the unity of the Trinity.

These basic schemata of history clearly indicate that Joachim has an economic view of the Trinity, that is, one which focuses on the works of the Trinity. His association of each Person with a temporal period is always made through the works which characterize that period. These works are generally associated with an order of the elect as, for example, in the case of the three epochs and the times of the two Testaments. Book V, Part I, of the *Liber Concordie* is the most important text for understanding Joachim's division of history into seven ages. The most important texts for understanding the three epochs and two times are found in Chapters 4–10 of the *Liber Concordie*, Book II, Tract I, and in Chapters 5 and 6 of the "Liber Introductorius" of the *Expositio in Apocalypsim*. The latter text is a succinct summary of the text from the *Liber Concordie*, with the addition of a more complete discussion of the relation between the five times and three epochs. In both texts Joachim offers his reasons for the suitability of dividing history according to the three epochs and the times of the two Testaments, and the relation of these divisions to the Trinity.

In introducing the idea of the three epochs in the *Liber Concordie*, Joachim is well aware that this schema must be demonstrated by clear reasoning.[13] Consequently, he follows a carefully laid-out argument which may be summarized in five steps: (1) Using the Pauline distinction between the flesh and the spirit, Joachim distinguishes three types of lives led by the people of God in three different times. In the first time, from Adam to Christ, the people lived according to the flesh. In the second time, from Uzziah, king of Judah, to the time contemporary to Joachim, people lived according to both the flesh and the spirit. In the third time, from Joachim's time until the end of the world, people live according to the spirit. In the "Liber Introductorius," the abbot also characterizes these times respectively as a time of servitude under the law, a time of relative freedom under the letter of the Gospel, and a time of full freedom under the spiritual understanding. (2) Joachim notes that each time (*tempus*), which would be better called epoch (*status*), has a period of flowering and individuality. By this the abbot means a period when the works and the orders with which they are identified may be clearly perceived. The flowering of the first epoch was from Abraham to Zechariah, father of John the Baptist; the flowering of the second, from Zechariah to the forty-second generation (after Christ); the flowering of the third epoch, from the twenty-second generation after St. Benedict until the end of the world. (3) The abbot observes that the three epochs are distinguished respectively by the three orders of the elect. The Order of Married has its beginning in Adam and its flowering in Abraham; the Order of Clerics has its beginning in Uzziah and its flowering in Christ; the Order of Monks has a double beginning, in Elisha and in St. Benedict; its flowering is in the twenty-second generation after St. Benedict.

In the fourth step, Joachim offers several reasons for identifying each of these three orders with one of the Persons of the Trinity. His basic premise is that the Father, Son, and Holy Spirit work indivisibly as one God, yet as three Persons some works may be assigned to each. In a statement that reflects his awareness of the implications that the Sabellian heresy would have for an interpretation of history, Joachim asserts that if God were one Person three distinct works could not be sought nor could harmony be assigned in one work. Although numerous things have happened in the world, Joachim reasons, nonetheless God has so ordered those things one after another to show that there are three divine Persons. So that the individual characteristics of each Person may be understood, the image of the Father should be honored in those men who until the time of Christ were called fathers; the image of the Son should be honored in those who were redeemed by his blood and have been baptized by water and the Holy Spirit. As there have been groups of men in whom the images of the Father and Son were honored, argues Joachim, so there should be spiritual men in the image of the Holy Spirit, especially near the end of the world when the Lord will pour out his spirit on all flesh (see Joel 2:23). Joachim also reasons that the qualities appropriate to each of the three Persons relate directly to the purposes of each of the orders. As the Father is so-called because he has a Son, so the Order of Married bears the image of the Father because its duty is procreation. As the Son is the Word of God, so the Order of Clerics bears the image of the Son because its duty is proclaiming the ways and laws of God to God's people. The Order of Monks bears the image of the Holy Spirit, who is the love of God, because this Order is inspired by the love of God to despise this world and worldly things.

In the fifth and final step of his argument, Joachim connects the three Persons directly to the three epochs. Joachim's reasoning in making this connection focuses on the double procession of the Holy Spirit and on the double beginning of the Order of Monks. As the Holy Spirit proceeds from the Father and Son, so the Order of Monks proceeds from Elisha and St. Benedict. Joachim reasons that if the Holy Spirit proceeded only from the Father, as is appropriate for the Son, then the Order of Clerics and Order of Monks would have the same beginning and end. Here, however, Joachim shifts his terms from "orders" to "epochs." If the Holy Spirit proceeded from the Son, as the Son from the Father, then the third epoch would pertain only to the Holy Spirit as the second pertains only to the Son. But the Holy Spirit proceeds neither from the Father alone nor from the Son alone. Joachim is very taken with the idea that there is one divine Person (Father) from whom two proceed (Son and Spirit) and one divine Person (Spirit) who proceeds from two (Father and Son). Based on the logic of this relationship, Joachim reasons that the first epoch should be ascribed to the Father; the second, commonly to the Son and Holy Spirit; the third, to the Holy Spirit.[14] Nonetheless, Joachim states that the works of the second epoch are more appropriate to the Son, while the works of the third epoch are more appropriate to the Holy Spirit. Although indeed the Holy Spirit came in the second epoch (to the Virgin, at Christ's baptism, and to the apostles), his clarity was not that of the Son, who in the visible flesh rose from the dead. For this reason, Joachim states, Christ himself promised the sending of the Holy Spirit.

Joachim concludes his discussion by summarizing those things that may appropriately be related to the three epochs and the three divine Persons. The letter of the Old Testament is appropriate to the Order of Married; the teachings of the New Testament, to the Order of Clerics; and the Rule of St. Benedict, to the Order of Monks. Under another understanding, the Old Testament relates to the Father who is Unbegotten; the New Testament, to the Son who is Begotten; and the spiritual understanding, which proceeds from both Testaments, to the Holy Spirit, who proceeds from the Father and Son. The Order of Married, which was distinguished in the first epoch, is appropriate to the Father; the Order of Clerics, which is distinguished in the second epoch, to the Son; the Order of Monks, which is distinguished in the third epoch, to the Holy Spirit. According to all of these things, the first epoch is ascribed to the Father; the second epoch, to the Son; the third epoch, to the Holy Spirit.

To show that his idea of the three epochs is in harmony with the authority of the church fathers, Joachim asserts in the "Liber Introductorius" (5v-6r) that one may also speak of five times (*tempora*) of the world: before the law, under the law, under the letter of the Gospel, under the spiritual understanding, and in the full vision of the Lord. Joachim notes that the fathers spoke of the first three of these times, that is, before the law, under the law, and under grace. He finds it appropriate, however, to divide the time of grace into two periods, namely under the letter of the Gospel and under the spiritual understanding, and to add the "time" in the full vision of the Lord. The abbot notes that this fifth time is not a "time" in the true sense, since it is atemporal, that is, in heaven. The mystery of the Trinity is also revealed in these five times. Joachim points out that three of the five times are appropriate to each member of the Trinity, and shows why the first, second, and third times; the second, third, and fourth times; and the third, four, and fifth times, all may be ascribed respectively to the Father, Son, and Spirit: (1) The time before the law may be ascribed to the Father, since God allowed death to reign from Adam to Noah, revealing his awesomeness and inspiring fear in humankind. The time under the law may be ascribed to the Son, the Teacher and Legislator who illumines each person who comes into the world. The time under grace may be ascribed to the Holy Spirit, "for where grace is, law is abolished, and where freedom is, there is the Holy Spirit." (2) The time under the law may be ascribed to the Father, because during this time God spoke in many ways to the fathers. The time under the Gospel may be ascribed to the Son, for the Son appeared during this time, teaching and converting many to himself. The time which will be under the spiritual understanding may be ascribed to the Holy Spirit, because he teaches humankind all truth. (3) The time of grace may be ascribed to the Father, because spiritual sons are born to the Father through the action of the Holy Spirit, whom he had sent over Christ in the form of a dove. The image of the Father is here made clear in the sons. The time under the spiritual understanding may be ascribed to the Son, because what is finished in this time according to the spirit was first designated in Christ according to the flesh. The future age, after the Resurrection, may be ascribed to the Holy Spirit, because then souls will become spiritual bodies ruled only by the spirit. While these five times thus show the mystery of the Trinity, Joachim notes that this mystery is shown even more clearly when attention is focused on the times under the law, the gospel, and the spiritual understanding. These times are the three epochs. Joachim thus considers the three epochs to be in harmony with the three times of the fathers (before the law, under the law, under grace).[15] For Joachim the time before the law is simply an aspect of the first epoch. He presents the reasons for dividing the time under grace into two periods (under the letter of the Gospel and under the spiritual understanding) in his discussion of the relation of the three epochs to the times of the two Testaments.

According to Joachim, there is another way of viewing history that would divide history into two times according to the two Testaments. The time of the Old Testament began with Adam, flowered with Jacob, and ended with Christ. The time of the New Testament began with Uzziah, flowered with Christ, and continues until the end of the world. The abbot observes that these two times are characterized by two peoples, both having their genesis in corruption. The first people, the Jews, were a people of the flesh who followed Adam in sin. From them, fathers were chosen through law and circumcision. The other people were the Gentiles who, as St. Augustine notes, also began in corruption when an adulterer begat Romulus and Remus through the whore Rhea (LC 9r; see *De civitate Dei* XVIII:21). This people has sons through the sacrament of baptism. The image of the Father, the Unbegotten, is found with the first people, and the image of the Son, the Only Begotten, is found with the second people. The seven seals of the Old Testament and their openings in the New Testament as well as the lengthy discussion of the general harmony of the two

Testaments in Book IV, Tracts I and II, of the *Liber Concordie* are detailed discussions of these two times.

Joachim is very specific about the relation between the two times and three epochs. In the *Liber Concordie* (9r-10r) he bases the relation of these two schemata on the orders ascribed to the three Persons of the Trinity, again focusing on the double procession of the Holy Spirit. The image of the Father is found with the Jews, and the image of the Son, with the Gentiles. But so that images of the gifts of the Holy Spirit would not be lacking, Joachim explains that in the manner that the Holy Spirit proceeds from both the Father and the Son, spiritual men proceed from both the kingdom of the Jews and the Greek Gentiles. Even as the spiritual men (among whom were Elias (Elijah), Elisha, and the sons of the prophets) left the house of Israel and retired to the desert, so the fathers of the Greek Church also retired to the desert. As the letter of the Old Testament was entrusted to the Jews and the letter of the New Testament was entrusted to the Roman people, so the spiritual understanding that proceeds from both Testaments has been entrusted to the spiritual men.

In the "Liber Introductorius" (6v) Joachim focuses more specifically on the two Testaments and their relation to the three epochs. The abbot states that the time of the New Testament is double, because both the Son and Spirit have appeared in visible form: the Son in the flesh; the Holy Spirit in the form of a dove and fire. The Son was sent so that he might redeem the world, and the Holy Spirit, who proceeds from him, was sent so that he might complete what Christ had begun. The time of the New Testament, a time of grace, is divided into two periods so that in the resulting three epochs the works of each Person of the Trinity would be clearly distinguished. The abbot states that after assigning a double harmony between the two Testaments, it is suitable for a triple harmony to be assigned. What Joachim means by this may be clearly seen in Book IV of the *Liber Concordie*. The abbot follows his discussion of the general harmony between the two Testaments (Tracts I and II) with a discussion of the general harmony among the three epochs (Tract III). The division of the time of the New Testament into two parts does not make that time greater or lesser than the time of the Old Testament. Joachim here draws on an assertion of the equality of the three Persons. The abbot states that the Son and Holy Spirit together are not something greater than the Father alone, or less than the Son alone or the Holy Spirit alone. The relationship of the two historical schemata is thus a simple relationship of the New Testament to the Old, and the equality of the three epochs and their works. Thus simplicity may be perceived on the side of the two Testaments, and the likeness of the three Persons of the Trinity may be perceived in the works of the three epochs.

While the times of the two Testaments and the three epochs show clearly the works of the individual members of the Trinity, the seven ages of the world show clearly the unity of the Trinity. Joachim deals with the seven ages in Book V, Part I, of the *Liber Concordie*, in his commentary on the seven days of Creation. The exegetical method Joachim uses here is that of the seven typological understandings, each of which relates to one of the seven ways of confessing the indivisibility of the Trinity. In the abbot's commentary on Genesis 1 the seven days of Creation are the basis for dividing each of the three epochs into seven times. Thus under the first typological understanding, which relates to the Father, the first epoch is divided into seven times; under the second typological understanding, which relates to the Son, the second epoch is divided into seven times; and under the third typological understanding, which relates to the Holy Spirit, the third epoch would be divided into seven times.[16]

Joachim notes that just as there have been three understandings under which the three epochs have been divided into seven times, so there would be another understanding, common to the three epochs, in which the seven times of each epoch are comprehended in a single schema of seven ages (LC 72r). Thus the seventh typological understanding, which is appropriate at the same time to the Father, Son, and Holy Spirit, relates to the seven ages of the world. Here each day of Creation is an age of the world, these ages basically corresponding to St. Augustine's ages but with the seventh age being an historical age: Adam to Noah, Noah to Abraham, Abraham to David, David to the Transmigration to Babylon, the Transmigration to John the Baptist/Christ, John the Baptist/Christ to the present (Joachim's time), the present to the end of the world. Thus, St. Augustine, who is Joachim's authority par excellence, provides the basis for the historical schema which represents the Trinity's unity. There are, however, three other typological understandings that offer other ways of dividing history into seven ages. In the fourth typological understanding, which is appropriate to the Father and Son, the first six ages would be differentiated by ten generations, ending with Christ; the seventh age would be from Christ until the end of the world. According to the fifth typological understanding, which is appropriate to the Father and the Holy Spirit, there would be five ages up to Zechariah; the sixth age would be from Zechariah to Jovinian Augustus (fourteen generations after Christ); the seventh age would be from Jovinian Augustus until the end of the world. In the sixth typological understanding, which is appropriate to the Son and Holy Spirit, there would be five ages up to Uzziah; from Uzziah to the present would be the sixth age (sixty generations); the rest of the time until the end would be the seventh, Sabbath age (LC 73r). Joachim does no more than suggest briefly how these three understandings might be applied since, as he notes, they are seldom used. The first three and the seventh typological understandings, however, make clear the works of the three epochs and of the seven ages, which are appropriate respectively to the three Persons and to their unity.

The doctrine of election is crucial for understanding Joachim's vision of the consummation of history. The ordering of events and their contexts so that the harmony between them can be discerned as, for example, in the seven seals and their openings, provides the unity of history within which the operation of election can be perceived. For Joachim election involves not only the salvation of the individual but more importantly the successive calling of the elect and the movement (*translatio*) of God's favor from one people to another and from one order to another.

Joachim provides a general discussion of election in his *De articulis fidei* (Concerning the Article of Faith). The *De articulis fidei* is a short tract directed toward a monastic audience, written perhaps in the last decade of the twelfth century. Here Joachim briefly explains such tenets of faith as the Trinity, the Incarnation, the sacraments, and the virtues to be found in the monastic vocation. In the *De articulis fidei* Joachim's discussion of election is done in terms of individuals, but it shows the logic which Joachim follows regarding the election of peoples and orders in his scriptural commentaries.

Joachim focuses on Isaac's blessing Jacob rather than Esau as a model for election. He follows St. Paul (Romans 9) in holding that election is not by merit but by grace. The reversal of primogeniture is indicated to Rebecca even before the birth of Esau and Jacob. According to Joachim, this reversal indicates that election comes not through one's efforts but through God's mercy and compassion. For the abbot of Fiore, election is closely associated with abasement. He exhorts the monks to spurn those things which are valued among men and to stand in fear of the Lord, remembering that "many are called, but few are chosen" (Matthew 20:16). The monks should not, however, be preoccupied by excessive fear but they should learn through hope to expect mercy; their fear should function to help them choose humble things.[17] For Joachim the principle of election combines the ideas that the elder must serve the younger and that God casts down the proud and exalts the humble. In the larger contexts of history, this principle is seen in the movement of God's favor from the Jews to the Gentiles, and within the Gentiles, from the Greek Church to the Latin Church. It is also seen in the movement of God's favor from the Order of Married to the Order of Clerics, and from the Order of Clerics to the Order of Monks. The final work of history as Joachim envisions it, however, will be the reincorporation into the universal church of the peoples and orders that have thus been left behind.

Joachim notes that the two chosen peoples, the Jews and Gentiles, constitute one people of God. The Jews were called to bear sons according to the flesh, while the Gentiles were called to bear sons according to the spirit. Joachim's emphasis in his exegesis of the seven days of Creation as the seven times of the Old Testament (LC 61v-65r) is on the successive calling of the sons of Israel and their education under the law. In the first time, there was no distinction between the elect and reprobate, for all were without the law. But with the calling of Abraham and the sign of circumcision, the Lord distinguished Abraham and his decendants from other tribes who did not know God. For Joachim, the fact that each day of creation has an evening and morning signifies that the elect must pass through a time of sorrow before reaching a time of happiness. Abraham, for example, had to wander in a strange land for a long time; Jacob was made rich and famous only after his flight. In the second time, the Lord raised up the tribe of Levi so that he might be worshiped in the tabernacle and so that the Jews might begin to seek heavenly things. The Lord also separated the sons of Israel from the Egyptians and brought them into the promised land. In the third time, the Northern and Southern Kingdoms were divided and the Northern Kingdom was led into exile under the Assyrians. Those in the south who were left behind began to be educated in the law and to learn the words of the Books of Kings and the Psalms. In the fourth time, Elias, Elisha, and the sons of the prophets were called to instruct the people by spiritual example. Elias was lifted up to heaven so that he might return (at the beginning of the third epoch) and benefit the Christian people. In the fifth time, Gentile kings ruled over Israel, and the sons of Israel began to live with the Gentiles so that the Gentiles might learn the law of God. About the sixth and seventh times, Joachim is less precise than in his discussion of the sixth and seventh seals (see Chapter II). He notes only that in the sixth time the Jews returned to Jerusalem after persecution in Babylon, and in the seventh time they rested from their works, writing no scriptures. The creation of man on the sixth day leads Joachim to speak about Christ, the New Man, who with his Body, the Church, replenishes the earth and rules over it.

Commenting on the seven days of creation as the seven times of the second epoch, Joachim observes that the New Man, Christ, is the light sent to illumine the Gentiles and snatch them from the darkness of their ignorance. Darkness had been over the face of the abyss, he states, because the Gentiles had not known God and his law. But because the Gentiles believed in Christ, the inheritance of the Jews was given to them. In the second time, as a firmament was made in the middle of the waters, so the Church of St. Peter was placed in the midst of many peoples. Joachim notes that the Church separates out the elect, brings them into her bosom, and leaves the others behind. He states quite firmly that the Church of St. Peter, founded at Rome, receives and holds the elect in herself and that no one can be saved outside her. The works of the other days of creation lead Joachim to focus on the orders of the elect which characterize each of the times of the second epoch (pastors, doctors, martyrs, virgins, monks, new orders of laity). The larger theme of the movement of God's favor within the Gentiles from the Greek Church to the Latin Church is dealt with primarily in the allegorical sections of Book V of the *Liber Concordie*, in the *Expositio*, the *Psalterium*, and especially in the *Tractatus*.

According to Joachim, St. Peter brought forth through the preaching of the Gospel two Gentile peoples: the Greeks and the Latins. For the Greeks, Joachim has both admiration and disdain. He is well aware that it was among the Greeks that the early church was established and that the first clerics and monks were thus Greek. But the Greeks disputed with the Latins over the date of Easter, forcing Pope Victor I to excommunicate the Greek bishops. The Arian heresy spread among the Greeks and from the Greek tribes to Italy and infected the Latins. Not long after the death of Pope Sylvester I (d. 335), the Greeks left the Church of St. Peter and established their own authority in the patriarch of Constantinople.[18] According to Joachim, God's favor passes from the Greek churches to the Latin Church. Although the Greek churches are older, the younger Latin Church receives the inheritance through grace. In jealousy and indignation, the Greeks reject correct teachings, persist in their own errors, and keep truth from their lands.[19]

Joachim holds, however, that the great work of the third epoch will be the conversion of the Greek Christians and of the Jews to the universal Church of St. Peter. With the return of the Greeks to the true Church, the fullness of the Gentiles will be completed. Then, as St. Paul explains in Romans 11:25–26, Israel will be saved. Joachim asserts that as there was a light to the Gentiles at the beginning of the second epoch, so at the beginning of the third epoch, a light should go forth to the Jews. He finds it suitable that as once the Gentiles were converted through the Jews, so finally the Jews should be converted through the Gentiles. Joachim expected Elias to return at the beginning of the third epoch to aid in the work of evangelical preaching. The mission of the Church in the third epoch would be to carry the Gospel to the ends of the earth. With the completion of that work would come the final tribulation of Gog and Magog (Apoc. 20:8), the Last Judgment, and the Heavenly Jerusalem.[20]

The abbot also sees God's favor moving through the orders of the elect, giving preeminence in the Church first to the Order of Married, then to the Order of Clerics, and finally to the Order of Monks. In the second epoch, he sees preeminence given in the first four times to pastors, martyrs, doctors, and celibates. In the fifth time, the strength and numbers of these four groups increased in the Church. The sixth time of the second epoch, which Joachim considered to be his own time, was characterized by the emergence of the new orders of laity, such as the Knights Templar and the *conversi* of the Cistercian Order. These laity live under rules similar to the Rule of Benedict and use their talents to be of service to the clerics and monks. The abbot of Fiore attributed great significance to the calling forth of these laity by God. These lay movements were a sign that a new order was emerging which would gather together the diverse orders distinguished in the different times of the past. Organized under monastic rule, this new order would be dedicated to the task of carrying the Gospel to the ends of the world.[21]

This vision of the end of history is for Joachim a vision of completed symmetry and symbolic wholeness. When the third epoch had run its course, the works of the Holy Spirit would be clearly manifested as those of the Father and Son had been in the first and second epochs. The Trinity in all its dynamic relationships would be fully manifested in the historical process. Joachim's discussion of history in terms of the doctrine of the Trinity is simply a discussion of reality as he perceives it. One can look to the persons, things, and events of history to gain a correct understanding of the Trinity, because the Trinity provides the ordering principle of history. For Joachim the study of history is mediated by the study of Scripture and doctrine and remains but a step on the way to an understanding of the nature of God.

General Plan of Joachim's Four Major Commentaries

Exegesis According to the Letter

Introduction to the Study of Scripture:

Liber Concordie novi ac veteris Testamenti: Books I–IV

- I: Man (Nativitas Christi)
- II: Ox (Passio Christi)
- III: Lion (Resurrectio Christi)
- IV: Eagle (Ascensio Christi)

Exegesis According to the Spirit

General History/Old Testament Outer Wheel	General History/New Testament Inner Wheel
Liber Concordie: Book V	*Expositio in Apocalypsim*
I: 7 Days of Creation	I: Pastors
II: Genesis/Exodus	II: Martyrs
III: Four Books of Kings	III: Teachers
	IV: Hermits and Virgins
	V: General Church
	VI: New Orders of Laity
	VII: Rest
	VIII: Heavenly Jerusalem
Four Special Histories Old Testament	Four Special Histories New Testament
Liber Concordie: Book V, Part IV	*Tractatus super Quatuor Evangelia*

| Job ———————— Man (Nativitas Christi) ———————— Matthew |
| Tobit ———————— Ox (Passio Christi) ———————— Luke |
| Judith ———————— Lion (Resurrectio Christi) ———————— Mark |
| Esther ———————— Eagle (Ascensio Christi) ———————— John |

Summary: Book V, Part V   Minor Prophets
Book V, Part VI   Major Prophets

Trinity

Psalterium decem chordarum

- I: Psaltery (Contemplation of the Trinity)
- II: Number of Psalms (Works of the Trinity)
- III: Institution of the Psalms (Praise of the Trinity)

Liber Concordie novi ac veteris Testamenti

Tractatus super Quatuor Evangelia

Edited by E. Buonaiuti. Rome: Tipografia del Senato, 1930.

Liber Introductorius in Apocalypsim

Venice, 1527; reprint ed., Frankfurt/M: Minerva, 1964.

Psalterium decem chordarum

76

CHAPTER V

The Five
Great Works of Christ

J OACHIM OF FIORE'S writings are replete with images of Christ. In
the Incarnation, Christ humbled himself, taking on human flesh in
the form of a servant. He suffered rejection and ultimately crucifixion. He became a scandal such that people have found it difficult
to believe that he could be true God. Christ is the New Man, the Spiritual
Man, the Second Adam, the True Moses. He is the Son of God who has
conformed others to his image and has made them sons of God through
adoption. Christ is the Word of God become flesh, the Lion from the Tribe
of Judah who through his resurrection has achieved a great victory over
death. He has revealed many things and opened the seven seals. Christ is
the Bridegroom of the Church. He is the guide and companion on the pilgrim's journey. Joachim uses these conventional images of Christ to help
define the works of Christ from his First Advent in the Incarnation to his
Second Advent for Judgment.

The uniqueness of Joachim's understanding of the works of Christ
emerges when those works are examined in the context of the trinitarian
doctrine and scriptural commentary that constitute his theology of history.[1] For the abbot the central image of Christ is that of the Only Begotten Son who, with the Holy Spirit, was sent by the Father into the
world. Joachim finds significance in the fact that the Son and Spirit are
the two Persons of the Trinity who are sent, and in his discussion of trinitarian doctrine in the *Psalterium*, he explains the terms and meaning of
this sending (*missio*). For the abbot, the works of these two Persons in
history are a function of their mission for the salvation of the world: Christ
in assuming human flesh reconciles people with God, reforming them to
his image; the Holy Spirit makes the work of Christ effective in the hearts
of believers and reveals the mysteries of Christ.

Because the Son and Spirit are sent and reveal something of themselves to humanity, they demand a many-leveled understanding. To dis-

cern the working of the Son and Spirit in history requires the use of the spiritual senses of Scripture. But here Joachim's use of allegory and typology is informed by a principle laid down by St. Augustine (*De Trinitate* I:11): some things were written in Scripture with regard to Christ's human nature and other things with regard to Christ's divine nature. For the abbot the works of the Holy Spirit complement the works of Christ according to one or the other of these two natures. This complementarity is especially clear in Joachim's interpretation of biblical saints who are either types of Christ or of the Holy Spirit. A key text is Book III, Tract I, of the *Liber Concordie*, where he examines seven pairs of Old Testament saints, one person in each pair representing Christ and the other, the Holy Spirit. Through his interpretation of each pair, Joachim sets forth his understanding of the works of the Son and of the Spirit, an understanding determined by constant reference to that which is proper to Christ's divine and human natures. His other discussions of saints and symbols that represent the works of these two Persons of the Trinity follow the basic lines laid down in this text. In his scriptural commentary, Joachim shows that the works of Christ and the works of the Holy Spirit in the history of salvation constitute a carefully ordered symmetry.

In the *Psalterium decem chordarum* I:3–6, Joachim discusses the ways in which the Father, Son, and Holy Spirit are to be seen as three distinct and complete Persons. In his consideration of the Son and Holy Spirit, Joachim emphasizes their mission, reflecting the coalescence in his mind of several ideas gleaned from St. Augustine's *De Trinitate* II:5–6 and IV:20–21. The bishop of Hippo defined mission as the coming forth from the Father and coming into the world. He paralleled the sending of the Son to his generation from the Father, and the sending of the Holy Spirit to his procession from the Father and the Son. It is axiomatic for both St. Augustine and Joachim that the visible, temporal mission of the Son and Spirit should reveal the eternal relations that hold among the three divine Persons.

For the abbot of Fiore the sending of the Son and the sending of the Spirit are the focal points of the self-revelation of God, for they are the archetypal instances of the invisible made visible and the unknowable made knowable. These two Persons have assumed the bodily creature (*corporea creatura*): Christ took on human flesh in the form of a servant and the Holy Spirit appeared in the form of a dove and in tongues of fire so that each might be shown to humanity. For Joachim the bodily creature assumed by each Person is essential not only for the manifestation of the deity in a form understandable to limited human capabilities, but also for the completion and perfection of the work each Person was sent to do (PDC 238r).

The importance of the sending of the Son and Spirit for Joachim is emphasized by the fact that he enumerates five relations among the three Persons based on their mission. Joachim describes these relations on the principle that the one who is sent has a relationship to the one by whom he is sent. (1) The Father has a relation to both the Son and Spirit because they are sent by him from whom they have their being. (2) The Father and Son have a relation to the Holy Spirit because they send and give him. (3) The Son and Spirit have a relation to the Father because they are sent by him. (4) The Holy Spirit has a relation to the Father and Son because he is sent by them. (5) All three have a relation to the seven gifts, which are called the seven spirits of the Lord, and to each creature, and especially to their messengers. According to the abbot, these relations began with time when the creatures existed to whom the Son and Spirit were sent, and to whom the seven spirits of the Lord were sent by them. Joachim is clear here that these are temporal relations based on mission and should not be understood as either the eternal generation of the Son or the procession of the Spirit (PDC 261v-262r). Yet the connection between generation, procession, and mission is so close in Joachim's mind that he does not consistently distinguish them when describing the relations among the three Persons. In an earlier description of the five eternal relations that hold among the divine Persons (257v), for example, Joachim gives the fourth relation as that which the Holy Spirit has to the Father and Son because he is sent by both, a relation which would properly be based on procession rather than mission.[2]

In his comments on the figure of the Psaltery of Ten Strings, Joachim notes that in some mystical figures that which is sharp may indicate a beginning or an end. By a beginning should be understood that from which the point originates, and by an end, there where the point finishes. But the abbot distinguishes between being a beginning or an end, which for him pertains to eternity, and having a beginning or an end, which for him pertains to temporality. Omnipotent God is a beginning because he has created all things from nothing. God is an end because all the works which were begun by him come to perfection through him and find their consummation in him. Each of the three Persons may also be called a beginning: the Father is the beginning of the Son and Spirit; the Son with the Father is the beginning of the Spirit; the Spirit is the beginning of the Son with regard to his human nature, as the man Jesus was conceived by the Holy Spirit. Thus all three corners of the Psaltery might be described as a beginning. But Joachim considers that this might lead to confusion: one might think that the Son and Spirit were the beginning of the Father, or that the Father and Spirit were the beginning of the Son with regard to his divine nature. Consequently the abbot designates the blunted top of the Psaltery as a beginning and the two lower, pointed corners as ends (see Figure V; PDC 237v-238v).

The abbot of Fiore finds several meanings in the blunted corner at the top of the Psaltery. He has designated it a beginning, for while it begins from nothing, it is itself a beginning of the Son and Spirit. The corner's lack of a sharp point indicates the eternity which is fitly ascribed to the Father. Its width indicates that the eternity of the Father is shared with the Son and Spirit through their divine nature. God as Trinity is beyond temporality, for there is no change in divinity. The lack of a point also indicates that the Father was not alone before the creation of the world. Together with the Son and Spirit, the Father created all things. Here Joachim interprets the bluntness of the top of the Psaltery to indicate creation from nothing.

Joachim has designated the two lower corners, which signify the Son and Spirit, as ends. Because the Son and Spirit assumed the bodily creature and appeared in visible form to humankind, they have entered the temporal realm and thus have an end. The abbot explains that the Son and Spirit do not cease to be, but the works associated with their temporal mission do cease. The Son has an end because the temporal life which he took on by assuming human flesh ceased. He will have an end when his body, the Church, ceases to exist. The Holy Spirit will have an end when the effusion of his gifts ceases, as did the meal and oil pouring forth from the jars filled by Elias for the widow woman (I Kings 17). Indeed, the end of the work of the Trinity is shown in the two lower corners. For the Son and Spirit were sent in visible form into the world by the Father so that the awesomeness which the Father revealed in himself might be mercifully softened in them. But the work of the Son and Spirit for the redemption of humankind will only be completed at the end of the ages (PDC 238v-239r).

The work of the Son and Spirit for the redemption of humankind is also shown in the ten chords of the Psaltery. On the left side, which shows the generation and sending of the Son, the chords are labeled according to the nine choirs of angels. The lowest rank, angels, is represented in the bottom chord; man is represented in the tenth and highest chord.[3] Joachim considered that in assuming human form the Son became lower even than the angels. But in redeeming humankind, Christ raised man back above the angelic ranks. On the right side of the Psaltery, which shows the procession and sending of the Spirit, the ten chords are labeled according to the seven gifts of the Spirit and the three theological virtues. Fear of the Lord (*timor domini*) is represented in the bottom chord, while Wisdom (*sapientia*) is represented in the seventh chord. Faith, Hope, and Love are represented in the eighth, ninth, and tenth chords. Joachim holds that the Holy Spirit also humbled himself in descending to the world. But through the seven gifts and the infusion of the three virtues into the hearts of the elect, the Holy Spirit works to raise man back to God.

The abbot distinguishes between the kind of humility shown by the Son and that shown by the Holy Spirit. Joachim holds to the christological doctrine of the two natures in one person: in assuming the bodily creature, the Son took humanity into the unity of his person. The Holy Spirit did not assume the bodily creature into his person. Rather, by appearing in the form of a dove and in tongues of fire, the Spirit revealed in visible form the simple divine nature. The Son, then, according to his human nature was more humbled than the Holy Spirit.

Because both the Son and the Spirit have assumed visible form and have come into the world, Joachim asserts that they require a many-leveled understanding with regard to the saints and symbols that represent them. He makes this idea more explicit with regard to the two natures of Christ. The abbot follows a well-established exegetical tradition in distinguishing between those works that are to be referred to Christ's human nature and those that are to be referred to his divine nature. According to his human nature, for example, Christ was conceived by the Holy Spirit and thus the Spirit may be seen as his beginning. According to his divine nature, Christ sends the Spirit and may be seen as a beginning of the Spirit. For Joachim this is a distinction rooted in the idea of *proprietas*: some things are by their very nature proper to Christ's human nature; others, to his divine nature. Christ's humiliation is proper to his human nature; his glorification, to his divine nature. Those works that by their very nature are proper to the Holy Spirit provide an appropriate complement to these works of Christ.

This principle of distinction based on the trinitarian idea of *proprietas* guides Joachim as he uses allegory and typology to interpret biblical passages with regard to the works of Christ and of the Holy Spirit. The most important text for understanding the relation between these two Persons is in Book III of *Liber Concordie*, which is devoted to the seven seals and their openings. In Tract I (25r-38v) Joachim discusses the Old Testament saints whose lifetimes mark the specific times represented by each of the seals. Abraham, Isaac, and Jacob mark the beginning of the first seal and are followed by seven pairs of men: Joseph/Manasseh, Moses/Joshua, Samuel/David, Elias/Elisha, Isaiah/Hezekiah, Ezekiel/Daniel, and Joshua, son of Jehozadak/Zerubbabel. Abraham, Isaac, and Jacob designate the Trinity; in each pair of men one person designates Christ while the other designates the Holy Spirit. The relation between the men in each pair provides an analogy to some aspect of the relation between Christ and the Holy Spirit. The pattern of interpretation that is represented in this text is found throughout Joachim's scriptural commentary.

The abbot of Fiore begins his interpretation by paralleling the three men who visited Abraham to the three patriarchs, and the two angels sent to Sodom and Gomorrah to the series of seven pairs of Old Testament saints. Three men equal in all respects appear to Abraham who was residing on the height of the Mamre Valley because there are three Persons of the Trinity who remain on the height of majesty. Yet as two angels are sent down to Sodom and Gomorrah, so the Son and Spirit are sent into the world for the purpose of saving the elect or condemning the reprobate. Joachim finds it fitting that the three patriarchs mark the beginning of the series of pairs of saints. Abraham, Isaac, and Jacob bear the type of the almighty God who is three and one and begin the series of saints because "the stable and unshakeable confession of the holy and indivisible Trinity is the foundation of the Christian faith" (LC 27r). But equally a part of the Christian faith is the sending of Christ and the Holy Spirit to the world. Joachim warns that the humility of these two Persons of the Trinity should not be a stumbling block to faith. The seven pairs of saints, he asserts, were chosen by God so that they would bear the type of those who work through them. Thus, of each pair, one person bears the type of Christ and one bears the type of the Holy Spirit.

Joachim observes that the pairs of saints are so ordered that in each pair, with the exception of Joshua, son of Jehozadak/Zerubbabel, one person is preferred to the other. For example, Moses, who signifies Christ, is preferred to Joshua, who signifies the Holy Spirit. In three pairs (Moses/Joshua, Elias/Elisha, Ezekiel/Daniel), the person signifying Christ is preferred to the person signifying the Holy Spirit; in three pairs (Joseph/Manasseh, Samuel/David, Isaiah/Hezekiah), the person signifying the Holy Spirit is preferred to the person signifying Christ; in the final pair (Joshua, son of Jehozadak/Zerubbabel), the two men are equal. This numerical equality of preferences testifies, Joachim argues, to the "equality and co-eternal majesty" of the Son and Spirit. Through his interpretation of these pairs of saints, Joachim explains the manifold understanding of the Son and Spirit. He relates the pairs Joseph/Manasseh and Moses/Joshua to the work of Christ and the Holy Spirit in accomplishing salvation. His discussion of the remaining five pairs of men centers on the work of Christ and the work of the Spirit within the Church.

Although the first pair of men is Joseph and Manasseh, Joachim focuses his discussion on the relation between Manasseh and Ephraim. The abbot is fascinated by the interchange between Jacob, Jacob's son Joseph, and his grandsons Manasseh and Ephraim regarding the conferral of the elder patriarch's blessing. Joseph brings his sons to Jacob's sickbed for a blessing, and Jacob blesses the younger Ephraim with his right hand and Manasseh with his left hand, reversing the appropriate order (Genesis 48). For Joachim this reversal of primogeniture, like that of Jacob and Esau, serves as a model for understanding the passing of God's favor from one group to another, for example, from the Jews to the Gentiles. Here the abbot interprets the interchange with regard to the relation between the Son and Spirit. Jacob bears the type of God the Father; Joseph and Ephraim, the type of the Holy Spirit; and Manasseh, the type of Christ. More specifically, Joseph signifies the Person of the Spirit while Ephraim signifies the grace and fruit of the Spirit; Manasseh signifies the humanity of Christ (LC 27r–29r; EA 49v).

Joachim first points out the implications of the transferral of blessing and preference to Ephraim according to the letter of Scripture. Manasseh and Ephraim are equal, he notes, and yet Manasseh is preferred to Ephraim by order, Ephraim is preferred to Manasseh by grace. Manasseh did not squander or lose his first-born rights and yet a blessing was conferred on Ephraim indicating that the last would be first and the first, last.

Manasseh is first by birth and Ephraim is first by grace so that they might learn to honor each other.

According to the spirit of Scripture this relation between Manasseh and Ephraim has implications for the relation between Christ and the Spirit. On a very basic level Joachim enumerates a number of things that follow this pattern of preference: one looks first to law, then to grace; first to the baptism of water that John preached, then to the baptism of fire and the Spirit that Christ promised; first to the nativity of the Lord, then to the resurrection. In all of these things the first are humble, the second, more excellent. But for Joachim the crux of this relationship is the willing humility of Christ, signified in Manasseh, in the face of the glory of the Holy Spirit, signified in Ephraim. Who but Christ, the abbot asks rhetorically, would willingly submit himself to the part of Manasseh, taking the form of a servant and the lesser part in all things so that he might redeem humanity and so that the grace of the Holy Spirit might then work in the elect.

Joachim offers here a meditation as it were on this work of Christ in accepting humiliation for the redemption of humanity. Christ was born from a woman so that people would be born from God. He was baptized by water so that they could be baptized by the Spirit. He was humbled to earth so that humanity could be raised to heaven. He was surrendered to death so that people could be raised to eternal life; he was made an outcast so that they would be led back to their fatherland. Christ undertook the passion from the left hand of God the Father so that the right hand of the Father could snatch humanity from passion.

In the *Expositio in Apocalypsim* (32r-v) Joachim continues in a similar manner, detailing more specifically the relation between the humanity symbolized in Manasseh and the gifts of the Spirit symbolized in Ephraim. Each part of the human body that Christ assumed merited one of the spiritual gifts for humanity. Christ took on human weakness so that he might convey his power to humanity. He received sight so that he might give the spirit of wisdom which illumines the inner eyes. He received hearing so that he might give the spirit of understanding which opens the inner ears. Christ had the sense of smell and gave the spirit of counsel which imparts spiritual discrimination. He had the power of speech and gave the spirit of knowledge. Christ had hands and gave the spirit of fortitude, he had feet and gave the spirit of piety, and he had the weakness and suffering of a mortal body and gave the spirit of fear (*timor*). This symbolism is included in the monastery plan of the *Liber Figurarum*, each oratory represented by one part of the body and by one of these seven spirits (see Figure III and discussion in Chapter II).

The abbot of Fiore also finds significance in the meaning of the names "Manasseh" and "Ephraim." Manasseh means forgetfulness (*oblivio*), because Christ, who was born and taught among the Jews, teaches his elect to forget the law of Moses, which is a law of the flesh. Ephraim means fruitfulness (*fructificatio*), for the fruits of righteousness, the gifts of the Spirit, prosper in the tribe of Ephraim, which represents the Gentile people. Christ was humbled among the Jews so that the Holy Spirit might bear fruit among the Gentiles.

Joachim finds the greatest example of humility in the humanity of Christ, but the grace imparted through the action of the Holy Spirit is necessary for the growth of the fruit of the Spirit (which has been won through the humanity of Christ). The abbot connects the virtue of humility to the humanity of Christ and the virtue of love to the gracious action of the Holy Spirit. Both of these virtues are excellent and each requires the other.[4] In the humility of the Incarnation, for example, Christ gave to the Church his flesh in the sacrament of his body and blood. But unless love is present, this sacrament is received for judgment and not for salvation. Here the love of God which is poured out in the hearts of the elect is preferred to the form of a servant which Christ assumed. In this aspect of his work, Christ wished the Holy Spirit to be preferred to himself (LC 28v).

Joachim finds the evidence that Christ wished the Holy Spirit to be preferred to himself in Philippians 2:6 and John 16:7. In Philippians 2:6, Paul observes that Christ, although in the form of God, did not hold on to his equality with God but emptied himself in the form of a servant. For Joachim, this undoubtedly is underlined by St. Augustine's observation in *De Trinitate* that Christ, although equal to God in his divine nature, may be seen as less than God according to his human nature, in the form of a servant. In John 16:7, Christ himself observes that unless He goes away, the Paraclete cannot come; if, however, He leaves, He will send the Paraclete.[5] Christ's humiliation and departure, according to Joachim, are so entirely necessary for the sending of the Spirit, that without them the Spirit cannot come. The abbot further illustrates this with the example of Joseph trying to place Jacob's right hand on Manasseh rather than Ephraim. Just as Joseph wished to secure the preference for Manasseh, so God the Father, wishing to glorify the despised Christ, made signs and miracles in

Jerusalem where Christ had suffered. But Jacob refused to bless Manasseh with his right hand; and the wish of God the Father did not prevail, or the gift of the Spirit might have been lost because flesh had not been sufficiently humbled. For Joachim, a glorification in the flesh is impossible. Indeed, a total humiliation of the flesh must precede the reception of the Holy Spirit. Christ assumed human nature so that he would be despised, not so that he would be glorified. On the level of his human nature, Christ remains less than the Holy Spirit. It remains for the next pair of figures, Moses and Joshua, to illustrate the mode of glory of Christ in preference to the Holy Spirit.

Moses bears the type of Christ and is preferred to Joshua, who bears the type of the Holy Spirit (LC 29r-32r). The crucial incident in the lives of these two men, for Joachim, is Moses' laying his hands on Joshua. As Moses gives authority to Joshua and Joshua then enters the promised land for Moses, so after his ascension Christ gives authority to the Holy Spirit and the Holy Spirit then enters the world. For Joachim the meaning of John 16:7 is completed in John 16:13–14. Christ departs and ascends to the Father and only after His ascension does Christ send the Spirit. What the Spirit speaks and declares is by the authority of Christ and will glorify Christ. The glorification of Christ is thus entirely apart from the flesh. According to Joachim, the authority which on a human level Joshua receives from Moses through the laying on of hands, the Holy Spirit receives from Christ through their shared eternal nature.

The authority given to the Holy Spirit by Christ has implications for Joachim's idea of the spiritual understanding of Scripture. Joachim notes that just as all eloquent speech may by its very nature be related to the Word, so the spiritual understanding may by its very nature be related to the Spirit. He orchestrates this relationship by pointing out a common biblical pattern: learned men come first and are followed by men less skilled in words but fuller in grace. Thus Moses, the erudite legislator, is followed by Joshua, about whom Scripture records little. St. Paul is followed by John the Evangelist who is unskilled in words but full of grace. Christ himself observed that unless he went away, the Spirit would not come. According to Joachim, it is as if Christ meant to say, "Unless I remove the worship of speech, on which the carnal understanding feeds . . . you are not able to receive the spiritual understanding" (LC 32r). Nonetheless, in this context, the spiritual understanding, just as the Spirit who gives it, works by the authority of Christ, reveals the mysteries of Christ, and is meant to glorify Christ. Moses dies, and Joshua, his minister, enters the promised land; Christ ascends, and the Spirit is sent to reveal Christ's truths and glorify him. Joachim reminds the reader that in this discussion Moses, who bears the type of Christ, is preferred to Joshua, who bears the type of the Holy Spirit.

Of the third pair of men, Samuel, who signifies the Holy Spirit, is preferred to David, who signifies Christ (LC 32v). Joachim draws a parallel between Samuel and his mother Anna, and Joseph and his mother Rachel. Both women greatly desired sons but remained sterile for a long time. They were finally filled with grace and bore spiritual sons. Joachim notes that Samuel and Joseph, when seen together with their mothers, designate the spiritual sons of the church, or the fruits of grace. Samuel also designates the love of God which nourishes the love of neighbor. The biblical motif of "seven sons" designates the seven spiritual gifts which are poured out among the elect. Joachim states that Samuel, when considered apart from Anna, designates the Holy Spirit. Samuel was sent to the house of Jesse to anoint David king as the Holy Spirit was sent to anoint Christ. Joachim underlines the idea that anointing may be seen appropriate to the Holy Spirit. Although the baptism of Christ is usually referred to as "the Father anointing the Son with the Holy Spirit," one should not think that anointing belongs to the Father. Joachim observes that the act of anointing belongs to the whole Trinity; nonetheless, anointing and the pouring out of spiritual gifts is by its very nature appropriate to the Holy Spirit. As David at thirty years of age was anointed by Samuel, so Christ at thirty years of age was anointed by the Holy Spirit. In these works, as Samuel is preferred to David, so the Holy Spirit is preferred to Christ.

Joachim begins his lengthy and important interpretation of Elias (Christ) and Elisha (Holy Spirit) by noting that it is sometimes appropriate for Christ to be preferred in his own things to the Holy Spirit. Otherwise heretics might mistakenly suppose that the humility of the Incarnation means that Christ is lesser than the Holy Spirit. Joachim reminds the reader that although Christ may be seen as less according to his humanity, he is equal in all things according to His divinity. The abbot also points out the similarity between the pair Elias/Elisha and the pair Moses/Joshua. Elisha was a minister of Elias as Joshua was a minister of Moses. Preference goes to Elias (Christ) as it also went to Moses (Christ). Whereas Joachim focused on the relations between Moses and Joshua, he

discusses Elias and Elisha separately, focusing rather on the significance
of the individual characteristics of each (LC 32v-36v).

Elias' importance for Joachim is predicated on his expectation that
Elias would return at the end of the world, preceding the Second Advent
of Christ. Joachim thought that Elias' return would signal the final events
of salvation history and that Elias himself would lead the last crucial
thrust of evangelical preaching. Within the context of christology, Elias
takes on added significance since he prefigures the very nature of the
Second Advent of Christ. Joachim draws a clear contrast between John
the Baptist and Elias which he then applies to the First and Second Advents of Christ: John the Baptist precedes and prefigures Christ's First
Advent in humility, Elias precedes and prefigures Christ's Second Advent
in majesty and glory (LC 32v-33v; EA 54v-58r, 77r).

For Joachim the character of Christ's First Advent derives from the
fact that Christ assumed human flesh for the salvation of humanity. The
abbot notes that John the Baptist bears the type of the humanity of Christ.
The name "John" means "grace of God," and Joachim equates grace with
the humanity of Christ. John the Baptist's death at the hands of Herod is
a type of the crucifixion. Joachim finds John's remark, *"Qui post me venit
ante me factus est, qui prior me erat"* (John 1:15: "He who comes after
me was regarded before me, for he was before me"), quite appropriate to
a distinction in kind between Christ's First Advent in humility and his
Second Advent in glory. Christ's First Advent in the humble form of a
servant is within time, for temporality is a characteristic of humanity. His
glorious return, however, pertains to his divinity and is suitably placed
before his First Advent in humility, for divinity is extra-temporal. Joachim
notes that the Latin imperfect (*factus est/erat*) and present (*venit*) verb
tenses may appropriately refer to divinity, while the perfect, pluperfect,
and future tenses refer to humanity and almost never to divinity. The quality of mercy also pertains to humanity and thus to the First Advent.

According to Joachim, the character of the Second Advent of Christ
derives from the divinity of Christ which will be shown to all. The name
"Elias" means "my God" and indicates the divinity that is the nature of
the Word. The fact that the living Elias was taken into heaven signifies the
resurrection and ascension of Christ. Elias bears the type of the divine
Word, through whom all things were made. Joachim finds the genesis of
the Word from the Father (without a mother) an appropriate complement
to the birth of Jesus from the womb of Mary (without a father). The

marginal notes of the Venice edition of the *Liber Concordie* indicate that Joachim was relying on one of St. Augustine's sermons on the nativity of the Lord, but the quotation is in fact found in many of the Latin fathers, including Lactantius, St. Ambrose, and Pope Gregory the Great. Joachim quotes: "Who was born on earth without a father, himself was born in heaven without a mother, not having beginning or end" (LC 33r). The abbot connects justice with divinity and the Word. He finds it suitable that Elias comes before and after John. God wished to make known a love of justice and thus sent Elias first, so humanity might know from experience the righteous and awesome nature of God and thus make appropriate use of mercy and prepare for the final, terrible judgment. Joachim concludes that it is appropriate for both John and Elias to bear the type of Christ: Elias bears the type of Christ the Judge; John, the type of Christ the Redeemer. Both are one: the Christ who is about to come in the fire of judgment is the Christ who came in the water of redemption (baptism) that he might redeem humanity.

An interesting corollary to this discussion of the two Advents is found in the figure of the dragon with seven heads from the *Liber Figurarum*.[6] Here Joachim observes that Satan and the Antichrist imitate Christ in their works. Because Christ first came into the world in a hidden way, Satan himself conducts his work in a secret way in order to seduce the elect. And since Christ will come at the end of the world for Judgment and clearly reveal himself, so the devil will also come forth at the end of the world and clearly reveal himself. These two modes of the First and Second Advents also affect the final two Antichrists. The Antichrist symbolized in the seventh head of the dragon is hidden, as Christ's First Advent was hidden. The Antichrist symbolized in the tail of the dragon is the final and clearly revealed Antichrist, as Christ's Second Advent, which follows, will be. Thus even the persecutions that frame the seventh age, or the third epoch, are in harmony with those things that are appropriate to the two natures of Christ.

Joachim begins his discussion of Elisha by reminding the reader that generally only certain characteristics of each man are appropriate to the Person of the Trinity whose type that man bears. Seldom does every action of one Person enter into the typology. The abbot illustrates his point through an exegesis of Adam, who bears the type of Christ. Discussing the creation of Adam in Genesis 1:27, he shows that creation in the image of God appropriately refers to Christ; creation of man as male and female, to the Church; the animals of the sea, air, and land, to the three types of people (laity/clerics/monks) who make up the body of the Church. Having reminded the reader of the limits of what he considers an appropriate use of typology, Joachim is ready to consider in what respects Elisha bears the type of the Holy Spirit. He interprets the story of Elisha and the wealthy Shunammite woman and her son (II Kings 4:8–27) as an analogy to the work of the Holy Spirit within the Church. The abbot's comments on the events of the story prior to Elisha's raising of the dead boy concern the work of the Holy Spirit in the Church under the Old Testament; his comments on the raising of the boy and the following events concern the work of the Spirit in the Church under Christ.

In his comments on the early events of the story, Joachim emphasizes especially the shortcoming of the Law and the constant faith of a few believers in the grace of the Holy Spirit. The conflict that he sees between the Law and the Holy Spirit is especially clear in his interpretation of the visit of the Shunammite woman (Synagogue) to Elisha (Holy Spirit) in order to obtain help for her dead son. The woman first mourned that few people had the Spirit of the Lord. The woman asked for a servant to take her to Elisha as the Hebrew people sought mercy from God. The servant who drove the donkey quickly to Elisha symbolizes the order of prophets who wished to hasten the carnal Synagogue to the spirit of understanding. The woman threw herself at Elisha's feet, as the Church, seeing the futility of the ceremonies of the Law, joined herself to divine piety. Gehazi is sent ahead to place Elisha's rod over the face of the dead boy, as the scribe Esdra and other teachers of the Law tried to reform the heart of the people through the school of the Law. The failure of the staff to raise the boy is the failure of the Law to raise the people to a spiritual life. As Gehazi is forced to admit to Elisha his failure to raise the boy, so the priests of the Hebrew people, seeing the failure of the observation of the Law, are forced to admit that the flesh profits nothing but the spirit makes alive.

In his comments on the resurrection of the boy, Joachim stresses the work of the Spirit in bringing people to a spiritual life. Elisha came, entered the house, and stretched himself over the boy three times. The boy became warm, opened his mouth seven times, and revived. For Joachim, this event signifies the fullness of time when the Father sent the Holy Spirit in the name of Christ. The Holy Spirit entered the Church, warmed the sons of the Church with the fire of grace, and having lifted them up from eternal death, presented them safely to their mother, the Church. Elisha accomplished this miracle of resurrection after Elias had ascended, and the Holy Spirit works after the ascension of Christ to the Father. Joachim notes that the Holy Spirit is indeed another Comforter, whom the Father sends in Christ's name (cf. John 14:26) so that he might remain among the people eternally, accomplishing what Gehazi, the Law, could not accomplish. The abbot also directs his comments to the sacraments of baptism and anointing. Through the sacrament of baptism, the believer is baptized in the likeness of Christ, the name of the Trinity, and the power of the Holy Spirit. In the sacrament of anointing, the laying on of hands confers the seven gifts of the Spirit, symbolized by the seven times the boy opened his mouth. Joachim calls both of these sacraments kinds of "resurrections," noting that baptism is appropriate to Christ as it revives the body from death; anointing is appropriate to the Holy Spirit as it revives the soul from sins. When one is baptized and renounces Satan and all his works, one honors God; when the gift of the Spirit is given, as in anointing, one is honored by God.

Joachim comments only on II Kings 20 in his discussion of the fifth pair of men, Isaiah (Holy Spirit) who is preferred to Hezekiah (Christ). His remarks concern the passion of Christ and the sustaining comfort of the Spirit who aids Christ, and the believer, to pass through death (LC 36v-37v). Hezekiah, a king and the descendant of a king, was nonetheless afflicted with sickness because of his sins. According to Joachim, Hezekiah bears the type of Christ, the true King, who was weakened in the flesh for the sins he bore for humankind. Drawing support from Isaiah 53:4–5 and from St. Paul's remarks in Romans 4:24–25, the abbot emphasizes Christ's willingness to weaken and humble himself to death for the salvation of humankind whose flesh he had assumed. As God regarded the tears of Hezekiah, so he regards much more the affliction of the body of Christ. The fifteen years added to the life of Hezekiah are the fifteen virtues that contain the fullness of righteousness. Joachim divides these virtues into a group of seven (the seven gifts of the Holy Spirit), a group of five (humility, patience, faith, hope, and charity), and a group of three (work, reading, and psalmody). The elect are given these virtues by the Holy Spirit. The comfort given by Isaiah to Hezekiah is the comfort given by the angel of the Lord to Christ (Luke 22:43) so that he might be sustained through his passion and ascend into heaven. The Holy Spirit also works in this way in the elect. Moved by the Spirit, each believer learns to hate the world and to love heaven. The abbot observes that "he who presses death upon us also promises an anchor of hope in the resurrection" (LC 37r). For Joachim, the Spirit thus provides the sustaining virtue of hope, which enables the believer to pass through death and come through to life.

In discussing the sixth pair of men (LC 37v), Joachim directs the reader's attention to Pope Gregory's *Homilies on Ezekiel*, where the pope teaches that Ezekiel represents Christ. The abbot places Daniel among men such as Joseph, Joshua, and Samuel, all of whom are chaste and bear the type of the Holy Spirit. These men indicate especially the work of the Holy Spirit in the pouring out of spiritual desire (*spiritualis voluptas*) which moves people to despise carnal and unclean pleasure. A more important distinction, however, is that Ezekiel as a prophet remains surrounded by difficult puzzles, whereas Daniel as a prophet is much clearer. For Joachim this distinction touches on the relation between Christ and the Spirit, insofar as Christ observed, "I have many things to say to you but you are not able to bear them now; when, however, the Spirit of Truth comes, he will teach you all truth . . ." (John 16:12–13). Joachim draws a parallel between Ezekiel and Daniel, who were sent to the world for the salvation of humanity. Only the Father did not descend into the mire of the world; Christ assumed human form and was sent into the world; the Spirit was sent into the world in tongues of fire. Joachim reminds the reader that in this place Ezekiel (Christ) is preferred to Daniel (Holy Spirit).

According to Joachim, the seventh pair of men, Joshua, son of Jehozadak, and Zerubbabel, do not follow according to the models of preference but are valued equally (LC 37v-38r). Both were called to assist in the rebuilding of the temple of Jerusalem (Haggai 1, 2; Zechariah 3, 4; Ezra 4). Joshua, the son of the high priest, represents the Holy Spirit. He is suitably from the tribe of Levi, which lives more spiritually because of the rule of its order. Zerubbabel, the son of the governor of Judah, represents Christ. He is suitably from the tribe of Judah, the lineage of the Son of God. Joachim asserts that the structure of the temple pertains spiritually to Zerubbabel, as a leader of the people, while the sacrifice offered in the temple pertains to Joshua as a priest of the people. While the word of Christ gathers the elect into the structure of the Church, it is nonetheless necessary that the Holy Spirit remain with and among the elect continually. The Spirit offers a sacrifice to God for these elect so that He might kindle in them the fire of His love. Joachim concludes that it is entirely suitable that the series of pairs of men, each manifesting a preference for either the Son or the Holy Spirit, should end in this pair, which emphasizes again the equality of these two divine Persons.

Joachim's interpretation of these pairs of saints is typical not only of his use of typology and allegory but also of his logic in describing the relation between the Son and the Holy Spirit. The corollary to his idea of *proprietas*, that is, that some works are by their very nature appropriate to the human or divine nature of Christ or to the Holy Spirit, is the abbot's idea of "preference," that is, that certain works of one Person may be preferred to certain works of another Person without compromise to their equality. The details in the preceding interpretation of saints may be summarized under two general observations. With regard to the works of Christ and the Holy Spirit in the Church, Joachim asserts that the works of the Holy Spirit are preferred to the works of Christ with respect to the effecting of salvation in the hearts of believers. Christ accomplishes salvation by humbling himself in the form of a servant and the Holy Spirit brings this salvation to the elect. But what the Spirit brings and teaches in the Church is by the authority of the ascended Christ, and here Joachim asserts that the work of Christ in sending the Holy Spirit is preferred to the work of the Spirit in teaching the truths of Christ.

In his emphasis on and in a sense devotion to the humanity and humility of Christ, Joachim is reflective of the piety of his time and monastic culture. Devotion to Christ's humanity has been present in each Christian epoch but it gains a certain ascendency in the twelfth and thirteenth centuries. Like his contemporaries, Joachim's understanding of the Son of God has been gleaned from a thorough study and interpretation of Scripture, informed by the preceding tradition and enlightened by religious conviction that his mind had been touched by the illumining fire of the Holy Spirit. Always disdainful of the newly developing scholastic theology, Joachim has rejected de facto any notion of using philosophical distinctions or opposing arguments to clarify such points of doctrine as Christ's two natures and has appealed rather to scriptural and natural imagery allegorically interpreted. Joachim's theological method is clear even in minor tracts such as the *Adversus Iudeos* and *De articulis fidei*, in which his purpose is to establish the basic tenets of Christian doctrine and to defend or to explain them.

Standing in an exegetical tradition beginning at least with Origen, contemporaries of Joachim such as St. Bernard of Clairvaux and Rupert of Deutz found the Song of Songs an important christological text and extensively commented on it. Joachim, however, never comments on the Song of Songs and rarely quotes from it. That the abbot of Fiore would neglect such an important mystical text, which would seem on the surface to appeal to his imaginative mind, is indeed striking. Perhaps, it is Joachim's sense of the historical that makes him overlook the imagery of the Song of Songs in favor of saints and symbols drawn from the historical and prophetic books. As history in all its facets bears witness to the doctrine of the Trinity in general, it also bears witness to the relationship between Christ and the Holy Spirit in particular. This relationship is manifested not only in the details of the interpretation of each saint and symbol but also in the larger historical orders and periods which they may represent.

Important here is Joachim's assertion that the time of the New Testament is double because in it both the Son and Spirit are sent into the world. This time includes both the second epoch that pertains to the Son and the third epoch that pertains to the Holy Spirit. In Joachim's mind, the symmetry manifested in the doctrine of the Trinity that demands a time proper to the Holy Spirit also governs the relation of that time to the two preceding and especially to the second pertaining to the Son. The symmetry of the second and third epochs is conveyed through the models of preference. Indeed, if one looks at the works that characterize these states in terms of the logic or preference, which governs Joachim's understanding of the Christ/Spirit relationship, it is clear that the existence of a third state with works appropriate to the Holy Spirit does not imply the insufficiency of the works of Christ. The works of humility that characterize the second epoch are completed and glorified in the works that characterize the third epoch. Under the models of preference, for example, Joachim states that Christ himself left some mysteries unrevealed to His followers and prepared them to receive the spiritual understanding. This spiritual understanding, which the Holy Spirit pours out and which characterizes the third epoch, makes known all truth in Christ's name and glorifies Christ. Both Christ and the Holy Spirit are sent into the world, yet the Holy Spirit does not send Christ but Christ together with the Father sends the Holy Spirit. For Joachim, Christ's sending of the Spirit is in fact one of his five great works.

Ezekiel's vision of the wheel within a wheel (1:4–21) is a symbol through which Joachim pulls together the most important images that pertain to the works of the Son and the works of the Holy Spirit. The abbot understands the four faces of the living creatures to represent four great works of Christ: Man/Nativity, Ox/Passion, Lion/Resurrection, Eagle/Ascension. But to these four great works of Christ must be added a fifth. In the *Liber Concordie* (60v) Joachim observes that while the four works of Christ conform to the four faces of the living creatures, his divinity is only revealed in the fifth order of fire. In the *Expositio in Apocalypsim* (17r-v, 48r-v), he declares that the fifth work of Christ is the sending of the Holy Spirit in tongues of fire, fulfilling the promise of John 16:7ff. As each of the four works is connected symbolically to one of the Gospels, so this fifth work is connected symbolically to the Acts of the Apostles. Joachim's imaginative mind demanded that there be five works of Christ, for five is the number which pertains to the flesh, to the humility of Christ in the Incarnation; five is also the number of promise.

The figure of the *Rotae* (Wheels) based on Ezekiel 1 in the *Liber Figurarum* (see Figure IV) summarizes some of the symbolism connected in Joachim's mind with these five works of Christ. In the basic design of the figure, one face of each of the living creatures is associated with a small wheel that intersects the outer and inner "wheel within a wheel." The four small wheels are each divided into three sections, revealing some affinity in composition with that of the Trinitarian Circles (Figure II). In the *Rotae*, the Man, representing the Nativity of Christ, is on the right, while the Lion, representing the Resurrection, is on the left. The Ox, representing the Passion of Christ, holds the bottom position, while the Eagle, representing the Ascension, holds the top position. In this placing there is a symbolic juxtaposition of birth in the flesh with rebirth in the spirit, abjection in the Passion with glorification in the Ascension. The logical progression of the figure begins with the Man on the right and moves clockwise to the Ox, then the Lion, ending with the Eagle.[6]

Next to the face of each living creature is (1) a short statement explaining the work of Christ associated with that face, and (2) the general order of the Church represented by that face and associated with that work of Christ.

Christ by being born was made man, and from this many are made men	MAN	In the Man is signified the Order of Doctors

Christ by dying was made an ox, and from this many oxen are slain on the altar of Christ	OX	In the Ox is signified the Order of Martyrs
Christ by rising was made a lion and from this many are made lions by the fortitude of faith	LION	In the Lion is signified the Order of Pastors
The man Christ by ascending into heaven was made an eagle, and from this many chose to be eagles	EAGLE	In the Eagle is signified the Order of Contemplatives

Joachim's explanations reveal the *imitatio Christi* which characterizes his understanding of Christ's saving work: Christ conforms both Christians as individuals and Christians organized as groups to his image. In his statement on the Ascension, the abbot explains that "the man Christ was made an eagle." The designation "man" is missing in the statements on the Birth, Passion, and Resurrection. That Joachim deemed it necessary to emphasize the humanity of Christ in the work of the Ascension is consistent with his idea that the glorification of Christ pertains to His divinity and is revealed only after the ascension with the sending of the Spirit.

Of the three sections into which each of the four smaller wheels is divided, Joachim devotes the innermost section to the virtue manifested in each work of Christ. The virtue is stated in bold letters, with a short statement of the associated work, for example, "Here Christ suffered" surrounding it in smaller script. Manuscript D of the *Liber Figurarum* repeats in this section the order of the Church already mentioned in connection with each face and adds one of the four major prophets (Isaiah, Jeremiah, Ezekiel, Daniel). In the *Psalterium* (244r, 263v) the abbot makes clear the relationship between each virtue and work. Christ showed humility in deigning to be born in the flesh, and by His work taught Christians to consent to humility; through His Passion He taught his followers to act with patience; by His Resurrection He taught them to be strong in faith; and by His Ascension He instilled hope.

These four virtues are completed by a fifth virtue written in even larger letters across the center of the inner wheel: LOVE (CARITAS). In the *Psalterium* (262r, 263v) Joachim explicitly connects love with the fifth work of Christ, the sending of the Holy Spirit. Three of the virtues, those singled out by St. Paul (I Cor. 13:13) are related to the three works of Christ which occurred after his death: Faith/Resurrection, Hope/Ascension, Love/Sending of the Spirit. Joachim agrees with St. Paul that love is the greatest of the virtues. Love, the abbot states, can only be infused in the hearts of the faithful through the Holy Spirit. The inner wheel of the *Rotae* then summarizes the work of Christ that pertains to His First Advent, beginning in humility but ending with love in the sending of the Spirit.

CHAPTER VI

The Sustaining Influence of Joachim of Fiore

T HE spread of Joachim's writings and thought presents many formidable problems which have yet to be answered. His patterns and schemes, his exegesis of key Scripture, his multitude of symbols and numbers, his conclusions about the coming age of man's history would be corrupted, borrowed, and redefined by future generations.[1] To further complicate the dilemma, much of what he advocated survived underground throughout the troubled eras of Early Modern European history surfacing here and there in true or false form, sometimes to be subtly included in other writers' works and sometimes to be damned. Subtle borrowings from Joachim's ideas pose a most difficult task of evaluating his influence, and when his ideas are debased by the vast pseudo-Joachite literature, the task becomes nearly impossible. Approximately twenty-five different works were falsely ascribed to Joachim and many of these popular writings deviated significantly from Joachim's beliefs.[2]

The two pseudo-Joachite works most nearly accurate in their following of Joachim's ideas were the *Liber Figurarum* and the *De septem sigillis*. The authority of the visual representations found in the *Liber Figurarum* cannot be assigned directly to Joachim, nor can it be said with certainty that Joachim controlled the production of this important book. Arguments based on external and internal evidence suggest that the book of drawings was composed between 1227 and 1239 by a disciple or group of disciples of the first generation of Joachites. The evidence suggests that the work was produced originally at San Giovanni in Fiore even though the earliest extant copies are to be found in northern Italy and England.[3] Even so, the *Liber Figurarum*, a faithful depiction of Joachim's more important ideas, serves as a handbook and visual summary of Joachim's ideas. Marjorie Reeves, however, has argued that the *Liber Figurarum* is an integral part of Joachim's major works because the abbot conceptualized his ideas in symbolic form before he wrote. Because Joachim's mind fabricated a visual image of his main schemata before he was able to elucidate his ideas in written form, the drawings become the foundation to his work rather than the explanation that grows out of his exegesis.[4] Therefore, even though the *Liber Figurarum* was produced by a hand, or hands, other than Joachim's, it still should be included as necessary to the understanding of Joachim's own writings.

The authorship of the *De septem sigillis* is also debatable, but it, too, follows the abbot's principles closely. This treatise serves as a summary of Joachim's more extensive presentation of the seven seals and their openings in the *Liber Concordie novi ac veteris Testamenti* and the *Expositio in Apocalypsim*. In the *De septem sigillis*, however, there is little interpretation of the seals or their openings as the treatise simply lists historical events associated with the seals.

Three most definitely pseudo-Joachite works, which had widespread influence after the death of Joachim of Fiore, are the *super Hieremiam*, *super Esaiam* and the *Vaticinia de summis Pontificum*. The *super Hieremiam* and the *super Esaiam* are polemical in nature and attack the church and state of the thirteenth century. Frederick II is pictured as the Antichrist, and there is a difference in attitude toward the Church. These spurious writings denounced and attacked the Church with a vehemence, whereas Joachim carefully maintained his loyalty to the Church regardless of the implications of his patterns and ideas. The *Vaticinia de summis Pontificum* is a series of paragraphs that give an eschatological interpretation to the papal lineage. Some fifty manuscripts and twenty printed editions of this compilation survive. The *Vaticinia de summis Pontificum* was added to, "kept up to date," and revised down to the sixteenth century. After the thirteenth century, the listings anticipate the coming of the so-called *pastor angelicus*.

These and certain other pseudo-Joachite writings actually had a wider audience than did Joachim's own works. The *super Hieremiam* was composed in the 1240s and survives in approximately twenty manuscripts and three printed editions, Venice 1516, 1526, and Cologne 1577. The *Vaticinium Sibillae Erithreae* was written in the early 1250s and survives in some twenty-five manuscripts plus fragments of manuscripts. The *De oneribus Prophetarum* was completed about the same time as the *Vaticinium Sibillae Erithreae* and survives in about twenty manuscripts. The important *super Esaiam* was composed in the 1260s and survives in numerous manuscripts with one printed edition made in Venice in 1517. The *super Esaiam* is usually accompanied by a small collection of drawings called the *Praemissiones.*

The spread of Joachim's writings and ideas throughout Europe has been studied by Reeves and Bloomfield.[5] Although the penetration of Joachim's literature remains obscured in many areas outside of Italy, knowledge about the Calabrian writer was due to the popularity of the pseudo-Joachite texts and to the abbot's mixed reputation. The earliest mention of Joachim's books and treatises being brought north out of Calabria is found in the *Cronica* of Salimbene who relates that early in the 1240s a Florencian abbot sought refuge from Frederick II in the Pisa convent where Salimbene was living.[6] The abbot had with him "certain of Joachim's writings," which he wished to preserve from destruction. The addition of this literature to the Pisa convent caused a stir of study leading the convent's Lector, Fra Rudolph of Saxony, according to Salimbene, to leave the study of theology in order to devote his whole attention to the literature of Joachim of Fiore. Salimbene concludes by informing us that Fra Rudolph became a "great Joachite" because of this material.

As was pointed out in Chapter I, Joachim of Fiore's reputation as an expositor of prophetic scripture was known to the famous of church and state. Not only was the abbot known among the highest religious and political circles during his lifetime, his reputation was further increased by widespread publicity in the thirteenth century because of scandals associated with his ideas. From the fourteenth century on, however, Joachim of Fiore more often was seen as an "ancient" seer of prophecy, or at least an "ancient" authority of the prophetic writings of the Bible.

The study of acceptance of Joachim of Fiore's prophetic interpretations was attractive to limited circles in the years immediately following the abbot's death. In 1215, Joachim's notions about the Trinity, which he had published in rebuttal to Peter Lombard, were condemned. Although this controversy is mildly associated with his apocalyptic studies, the condemnation did tarnish his reputation to a degree. More importantly, his eschatological interpretations were being studied by interested scholars in England and France as well as in Italy and Germany.[7]

Although the chroniclers recorded that Joachim's ideas were discussed and that sermons elaborating on Joachite themes were preached, early and mid-thirteenth century men were more taken by identifying the

Antichrist and tabulating the expected period of tribulation thought to begin in the year of 1260.[8] Joachim of Fiore never precisely proclaimed the year 1260 as the date for such events to occur, although the number 1260 was highly important to his schema. In Joachim's time sequence, there was not an exactness of dates but rather an emergence from one epoch to the next based on a rough scale of 1260. That fateful year arrived, therefore, with great expectation among those who had become acquainted with Joachim's writings and ideas. Joachim's reputation diminished when the year 1260 passed without the expected results of some noticeable "sign" that a new epoch had arrived.

The event, however, that gave wide publicity to Joachim's ideas happened a few years before at the University of Paris in 1254–1255. For the first time, some of the underlying ramifications of Joachim's interpretations became clear when a Franciscan by the name of Gerard of Borgo San Donnino proclaimed that Joachim's writings constituted a new dispensation from God. The scandal at Paris was the result of a much deeper academic quarrel between the secular masters and the mendicants affiliated with the institution and was not merely a reaction to Gerard's claims.[9] This quarrel basically arose out of a power struggle which ultimately had to be resolved by the pope in Rome. Gerard of Borgo San Donnino, who was a minor scholar but a fanatic Joachite, burst on the scene of the Paris quarrel when he proclaimed that the new age had arrived, that the Old and New Testaments would be replaced by a new and third dispensation that would contain certain works by Joachim of Fiore. Joachim, of course, had never taught such a doctrine as that of a third dispensation. Gerard of Borgo San Donnino had apparently based his contention on Apocalypse 14:6, which tells of an angel descending, carrying a book of "the everlasting Gospel to preach to those on earth—to every nation, tribe, language and people." In Gerard's mind, this was the Eternal Evangel of the Holy Spirit come to control the new age. Gerard's announcement, and the furor it caused at the University of Paris, could not be ignored and added fuel to the controversy already smoldering at Paris. To proclaim a new revelation from God was indeed serious business, and almost immediately, the pope appointed a commission to meet at Anagni to examine both the works of Gerard of Borgo San Donnino and Joachim of Fiore. Details of this hearing are limited as Gerard's writings were destroyed after the commission's report. Gerard seems to have circulated the *Liber Concordie novi ac veteris Testamenti*, as written by Joachim, prefaced by his own

Liber Introductorius. The recorded charges against Gerard from Anagni show that he had intention to add other works of Joachim to this collection, and the record indicates that Gerard may have already begun to gloss one or more of Joachim's main works.

After lengthy discussions, testimony, and examination of Gerard himself, and the writings of Joachim, the commission at Anagni made their recommendations to Pope Alexander IV, who condemned Gerard of Borgo San Donnino's *Liber Introductorius* in October 1255. Joachim of Fiore's writings were not judged to be in error by the pope, but Gerard nevertheless spent the rest of his life in prison. At Paris, the secular masters did all they could to identify all mendicants with Joachim and Gerard, and eventually the scandal touched the entire Franciscan Order to the extent that their Minister-General, John of Parma, a noted Joachite himself, was removed from office in disgrace.

Joachim's authority as an exegete of prophecy withstood the European-wide scandal arising out of the examination by the commission at Anagni, probably because Joachim's authority was well established due to the prestige of his association with well-known kings, popes, scholars, and other leaders during his lifetime. In order to combat any adverse publicity from these events, the scribes who copied Joachim's main works habitually began to precede the *Liber Concordie novi ac veteris Testamenti* and the *Expositio in Apocalypsim* with Joachim's Testamentary Letter and a letter written to Joachim from Pope Clement III that authorized Joachim's studies.

Joachim of Fiore's grand design of history was rarely a surface feature of Joachimism during the centuries that followed the abbot's death. Rather, the most vocal adherents of Joachim's thought tended to select from his texts individual prophecies to lend legitimacy to their own beliefs. Perhaps the most potent of all of Joachim's ideas was the expected leadership of the third epoch. In the centuries following Joachim's death, several new monastic orders saw themselves as the "new men" of the new age—the Franciscans, minor friar orders, the Augustinian Friars, the Jesuits, to mention a few. Joachim's conception of the third epoch was that the existing structure of society was to be reorganized, and the existing leadership to be replaced by a new order of contemplative monks (see Figure III), including a *"pastor angelicus."* The first epoch had been led by the laity, the second epoch had been led by the secular clergy, but in the new age, the Holy Spirit would appoint a monastic order of contemplative monks to direct the affairs of church and state. As E.R. Daniel has shown, the goal of history is to realize the fulfillment of Christ's mission, a part of which is to achieve a functional society based on the Body of Christ as described in I Corinthians 12:14–20. Thus, an integral whole is accomplished by bringing together the secular and religious orders with the laity into a system where the *spirituales viri* and the *spiritualis intellectus* will be predominant.[10]

Frequently, these believers in Joachim's interpretations adopted the view that the transition to the new age would be guided by either an angelic pope or by a kingly political leader or both. The idea of a universal leader (pontifex) entered into the pseudo-Joachite works from other apocalyptic sources and became a part of the expectation for the renewal of the Christian faith in the third epoch.[11]

A good example of how the prophecy concerning the coming of "new men" could affect new religious orders can be seen in the controversies surrounding the Conventual and Spiritual Franciscans during the late thirteenth and early fourteenth centuries. The secular masters at the University of Paris were correct in associating Joachim's name with the mendicants, particularly the Franciscans. The Franciscans and Dominicans, as well as some of the minor mendicant orders, promoted the belief that Joachim's interpretations had foretold the creation of their brotherhoods.

Joachim's writings had pictured the last epoch of history to be led by a community of contemplative religious who were to be markedly different from preceding monastic orders because the monks of the second epoch had been imperfect. Joachim predicted the coming of twelve holy men who had been prefigured by the twelve patriarchs and the twelve apostles.[12] The ministry of St. Francis of Assisi a few years after the death of Joachim of Fiore caused later Franciscans to portray St. Francis as a special herald or emissary announcing the new age, just as John the Baptist had done for the second epoch.[13] St. Francis' saintly life and the charismatic imprint of the stigmata gave visible proof that prophecy was fulfilled. Even the great Franciscan Minister-General, St. Bonaventura, was attracted to mystical Joachite interpretations of St. Francis, which probably went all the way back to St. Francis' companion, Brother Leo.[14]

The Friars Minor perceived the divine purpose of St. Francis to be a complete *imitatio Christi*. Like the One he chose to fully imitate, St. Francis taught the Word and showed the example by which individuals gained salvation and the Church would be reformed. St. Francis and the

Friars Minor deviated significantly from established forms when they interpreted the *vita evangelica* to be an active life mingling with the people rather than remaining secluded in a cloister. Furthermore, the Franciscan interpretation of the *vita evangelica* was only a part of their definition of the *vita apostolica*, which importantly included a new and unique explanation of apostolic poverty.

The standard bearers of apostolic poverty became the so-called Spirituals within the Franciscan Order. Two great controversies came to the surface in the late thirteenth and early fourteenth centuries over the question of evangelical poverty. The first was an internal dispute between these Spirituals, who reinterpreted the Rule of St. Francis and developed a rigid definition of poverty, and the Conventuals, who reinterpreted the Rule of St. Francis and relaxed their explanation of poverty in order to better carry out the order's pastoral duties. The second great controversy, which included the external expression of the first quarrel, was that between the Friars Minor and the secular clergy and other monastic orders over the true *vita apostolica*. In reality, the root of both arguments was apostolic poverty, which was a problem of historical dimension as well as a problem of theology.

Mendicancy, especially as practiced by the Franciscans, threatened the very structure of the Church more than any other previous reform movement. With its backward thrust of "renovatio," and its forward eschatological expectations, the Franciscan movement was significantly different from traditional monastic conceptions of the perfect Christian life. The unique ideal of individual and corporate poverty was coupled with the assumption that an active life in the world inevitably led the Franciscans to build a sacramental and preaching organization separate from and in rivalry with the established Church.

The secular clergy questioned the legitimacy of Franciscan ideals about poverty throughout most of the thirteenth century, and it was perhaps human nature for the individual Franciscan writers to overreact to these attacks with counterarguments that bordered on heresy. The controversy came to a head in 1322 when Pope John XXII launched a major investigation into the writings of Peter Olivi, a well-known Franciscan Joachite in the Spiritual camp. Pope John XXII's investigation, however, was actually an attack on the larger issues facing the Franciscan Order and the Church.[15] In the broader sense, the question was ecclesiastical since it dealt with the place of the Friars Minor in the organizational structure of the Church. In another sense, the argument was theological and directed against the ideal of apostolic poverty since it denied that Christ and His Apostles had lived in absolute individual and corporate poverty or, for that matter, that Christ had ever taught the need for absolute poverty.

The Franciscans could not really claim an historical succession extending back through the established Church to Christ, thus the order had a problem of historical dimension. They had no authority and continuity in time, whether it be monastic or clerical. Their immediate predecessors were the itinerant preachers of the twelfth century, and their beliefs were some new exegetical interpretations that had not yet become standard among church theologians. Thus, the apostolic life perceived by the more radical members of the order was a way of life they believed Christ and His Apostles had lived (or should have lived). Further, this simple way of life they believed would be lived again in the eschatological future when Joachim of Fiore's third epoch would usher in a *novus ordo* of contemplative religious. An historical gap from the first-century Church to the late medieval Church was bridged by future expectation among the radical Spiritual Franciscans. Unlike other reform movements which had taken place within a continuous institutional tradition, the Franciscans were faced with the problem of historical justification.

The Friars Minor reflected two forces merging in the late thirteenth and early fourteenth centuries. One force was the intellectual tendency, after the Gregorian reform, to turn to descriptions of the apostolic community other than those found in Acts 4 (which was the standard before the eleventh century) as a model for reform. The other force was the new concern for the humanity of Christ expressed by evangelical spirituality in the twelfth and thirteenth centuries, which presented a new challenge to the traditional Church. These "*novi apostoli*," as Abelard had called them, were wandering preachers who described themselves as "*pauperes Christi*" and "*imitatores Christi*," and subscribed to a broader view of the *vita apostolica* than monks in earlier times. These forerunners of St. Francis, who frequently fell into heresy, saw the *vita apostolica* as an active life outside the walls of a monastery. They lived in poverty and begged, living what they felt was a literal interpretation of the Gospels. They were never concerned with specific theological doctrines but modeled their lives on new, self-interpretations of the Gospel in order to show an example to their followers.

The apocalyptic faith of the fourteenth century was beginning to twist the schemas of Joachim of Fiore into a dynamic of revolution replacing the progressive consummation of institutions outlined by the abbot. Joachim's poorly defined and roughly outlined world order of the third epoch was mistakenly seen as an imminent deliverance from existing institutions and the replacement of the secular clergy and society by contemplative monks led by a saintly pope or emperor. Because of this type of future expectation, the Spiritual Franciscans did not place their hopes on existing institutions or types to give historical dimension to their cause. Pope John XXII was aware of some and possibly all of these realities when he began his attack upon Peter Olivi in 1322 in particular and upon Franciscan teachings about poverty in general.

In the end, the Franciscans added legitimacy to Joachim's writings through their powerful preaching organization. They also set a pattern of historical and eschatological justification to be used in later centuries by other religious orders founded during or after the twelfth century, noticeably the Augustinian Friars and the Jesuits, to justify their order's mission.

Sharing the apocalyptic mentality of the Franciscans, the Catholic reformer John Wycliff, in *The Last Age of the Church*, quotes both Joachim of Fiore (actually pseudo-Joachite sources) and Peter Olivi to support his indictments against the Church in Rome.[16] Later, Wycliff's ardent supporter and follower, and the prominent patron of Lollard ministers, Sir John Oldcastle (Lord Cobham), was arrested by Henry IV for his anti-Church activities. Oldcastle was publicly tried by the Archbishop of Canterbury, which created one of the more sensational scandals of 1413. For someone like Lord Cobham, personal friend of the king, to be openly tried for heresy, caused lasting antipathies among Lollards and Catholics alike, and in the next century, John Bale, one of the more prolific English Protestant writers, compiled the testimony and edited the text of Cobham's trial as an example of martyrdom for English dissidents.

Another example of using Joachim of Fiore to lend authority to one's cause can be found among the Protestant reformers. Leaders of the Protestant Reformation carried the idea of the new age further by mixing it with an identification of Rome as the apocalyptic Babylon and the Pope as an agent of Antichrist, or as one manifestation of Antichrist. Reformation thinkers frequently appealed to the authority of ancient interpreters of Scripture. Joachim of Fiore was the "ancient" authority to many when it came to the interpretation of prophetic Scriptures. A good case in point is the early English Reformation beginning with John Bale.

When he edited the text of Cobham's trial, John Bale attached to the end of his work several translated passages that he attributed to Joachim of Fiore. The purpose of the "Prophecyes of Joachim Abbas" was simple.[17] Bale wished to prove by ancient, Catholic exegetical authority that the Lollard movement was a part of God's divine plan for Christendom. Bale's so-called quotations from Joachim of Fiore are not identifiable to us, but the fact that he chose to appeal to Joachim's authority shows the esteem in which Joachim was held by some sixteenth-century writers. To illustrate, he had Joachim state: "The churche of Rome shall be destroyed in the Thyrde State, as the Synagoge of the Jews was destroyed in the Seconde State, and a spiritual churche shall from thens forth succede, to the ende of the world."[18]

John Bale's works make copious use of Joachim and pseudo-Joachite citations and references. In his *Images of Both Churches*, written in 1550, Bale not only cites Joachim, he follows a muddled historical pattern of 7s and double 7s in a further attempt to show that the English Reformation was the culmination of Church history.[19]

This same general theme of Protestant church replacing the Catholic in Joachim of Fiore's new age was continued down to at least the nineteenth century in England. For example, Nicholas Bernard (d. 1661), the Chaplain to Oliver Cromwell, cites pseudo-Joachite references in his *Certain Discourses, viz. of Babylon (Rev. 18:4) Being the Present See of Rome*.[20] And, as late as 1836, Edward Bickersteth in *A Practical Guide to the Prophecies* cites Joachim of Fiore to support that Rome is Babylon.[21]

Secondhand knowledge about Joachim and his writings had consequences which extend even to the present time. One of the most enigmatic topics yet to be studied for instance, is the apocalyptic influences upon the Admiral of the Ocean Sea, Christopher Columbus. Columbus viewed the events of the Age of Discovery and colonization of the New World as the fulfillment of prophecy. He appealed to the authority of Joachim of Fiore on several occasions in the quasi-autobiographical *The Book of Prophecy* written near the end of his life and left unfinished. Columbus probably got his Joachite ideas indirectly from the fourteenth-century French Spiritual Franciscan Joachite, Johannis de Rupescissa, whose Joachite speculations circulated in written form and by word of mouth among the citizenry of the Mediterranean for more than a century.

The best summary of Christopher Columbus' apocalyptic interests are in John Phelan's *The Millennial Kingdom of the Franciscans in the New World*, the most important study of early apocalypticism in the New World. According to Phelan, Columbus became convinced probably from reading a combination of apocalyptic sources including the Joachite, that two things must occur before a new era of world history would be initiated by God. First, the Gospel had to reach all the peoples of the world; and second, Jerusalem had to be restored to Christian control (or at least the Holy Sepulcher). Columbus saw his mission as relating to both these goals, and he legitimatized his role by citing the ancient authority of Joachim of Fiore. His citations are not identifiable as belonging to Joachim, and Professor Phelan believes that Columbus was really paraphrasing from a variety of Joachite sources that he may only have heard about and never read. Dr. Phelan suggests that Columbus may have had some indirect familiarity with the writings of Pierre d'Ailly, the *super Hieremiam, super Esaiam* and/or the *Vaticinia de summis Pontificum*. Two other possibilities are the pseudo-Joachite *Expositio Sibyllae et Merlini* and the *Vade mecum in tribulatione* by Johannis de Rupescissa. He may have heard Joachite traditions discussed at the Spanish court as Arnold of Villanova, the great lay-Joachite writer, served as a diplomatic agent of James II of Aragon and his brother, Frederick III of Sicily.[22]

Columbus believed that his discovery of a route to the East enabled Christians to spread the Gospel finally to all inhabitants of the earth. His frequent reference to "opening the door of the Western Sea" was a metaphor to symbolize salvation based on John 10:9, "I am the door, a man will find salvation if he works his way through me." A further extension of Columbus' discovery related to the second goal of the repossession of Jerusalem.[23] It was Columbus' plan, and one which he promoted to the Spanish monarchs, to utilize the gold expected to be taken from the New World in order to capture the Holy Sepulcher and to rebuild Jerusalem in preparation of the Lord's Second Coming. On this he "quotes" Joachim of Fiore twice that Zion must be rebuilt by a man from Spain.

Joachite references are scattered throughout the literature of prominent men from the Middle Ages to modern times. Scholars have yet to undertake the definitive studies necessary to calculate the influence of the Calabrian writer. In the later Medieval, Renaissance, and Reformation eras, an encyclopedia of names such as Dante, Telesphonous, Wycliff, Huss, Bullinger, Bale, Jewel, Knox, and Munster are suspected of having been influenced by Joachite writings. In the early modern period of European history one can add the names of Benard and Manuel de Lacunza.

Professor Marjorie Reeves is currently preparing a study of Joachim's influence in the nineteenth and twentieth centuries. Indications are that Bickersteth, Schelling, Nietzsche, Jung, and Maitland all display subtle effects of Joachite thought. In recent years, N. Cohn, *Pursuit of the Millennum*, has viewed Fascism and Marxism as rooted in Joachite ideas, and the Nazi Third Reich as indirectly inspired by earlier Germanic Joachite thought.[24] One could probably make similar Joachite connections to the Puritan's concept of a "City on the Hill," in colonial New England, and the sentiment of Manifest Destiny in American history.

The problem in trying to assess the extent of a sustaining influence for Joachim of Fiore is that his historiographical conceptions and philosophy of history logically gave an impetus to modern ideas about man and man's destiny. A surviving underground seed of Joachimism would seem to have influenced Comte's three progressive ages of history, for example, but there is little proof that such was the case. Joachim created an aggregate of symbols all of which pointed toward a New Age which would be the fulfillment of prophecy in history. Joachim's ideas suggested an improvement in man's lot with the added dimension that such improvement was mysteriously a part of God's plan and that improvement would occur within human time. It was ordained that change would occur and that man would be delivered into a new age sometime in the foreseeable future. With the dissemination of these basic notions by wandering preacher-prophets, Joachim's ideas infiltrated most corners of Europe. Joachim's basic thought, however, has suffered from the popularity of the pseudo-Joachite works that made Joachim into a prophet himself. Thus, a widely read surviving body of literature is extant which is false to Joachim's own intent and thought.

Although several of Joachim of Fiore's basic patterns and interpretations can be isolated as influencing certain men or movements in European history, Joachim's greatest legacy was his historiography. Joachim's original view of a cosmic world order was fresh and it was sustaining. It became implanted into the minds of Western men and was nurtured by intellectual inheritance. His historiography was persuasive and ultimately incited diverse men to action.

The key to Joachim's historiography was that he studied prophecy to determine the outcome of events and to order those events, past, present, and future, into systematic thought so as to produce a clear and logical arrangement of history. Prophecy was a vehicle through which an understanding of all events could be grasped. In the purest sense, Joachim was a product of intellectual forces at work, in effect, fermenting before and during his own time. He firmly believed that biblical prophecy was inspired, that it was true, and that it had a purpose. Yet, that truth was obscured and had to have the sharpest scholarly tools of investigation and interpretation applied in order to pry out the information God had intended to convey to man. As noted in Chapter III of this book, the time process of progressive revelation was already conceived by early writers and more recently advocated by such thinkers as Rupert of Deutz and Anselm of Havelberg. Joachim interpreted the Bible in terms of old as well as contemporary methods but with new conclusions. His claimed "*spiritualis intellegentia*" was really what we would call a "sense of history." He had a unique ability and a fertile mind which enabled him to understand the future because the future was a part of historical patterns that he conceived from grasping the extended past.

R.W. Southern has placed Joachim of Fiore directly into the milieu of his time. Southern has made a good case that Joachim was first and foremost a Scholastic writer because of his technique and his desire to present an orderly arrangement for the whole topic of Biblical prophecy. As R.W. Southern has stated: "He (Joachim) thought that by diligent application he had reached a fuller understanding of Biblical prophecy than any earlier exposition. He had worked harder, and thought more, and submitted to a more rigorous discipline than others."[25]

Although he was disdainful of the developing Scholastic theology, Joachim did for the topic of prophecy, however, what other Scholastics did for their subjects of interest. He put the whole matter into order by a strict application of accepted scholarly apparatus from which he produced a logical sequence of results, but the end result was more than a systematic ordering of prophetic systems. Joachim's kaleidoscopic and powerful imagination produced the most comprehensive analysis of history in the Middle Ages.

What on the surface appeared to be a Scholastic treatment of a very large subject was in reality a large-scale explanation of the dynamic of history. With his historian's mind, Joachim could visualize what he felt was the entire cosmic plan of God, a plan with a clear beginning in Genesis that moved in a straight line to a finality at the end of time. He presented an outline of the main historical events, past, present, and future. To Joachim, unlike anyone else, the process fit together in his mind. He developed a vision from study and systematic thought processes. His historian's imagination led him to the logical conclusion that history's greatest age was yet to be lived—that somehow change was the very fabric of history. Whereas the medieval Church and the medieval conception of history was seen by others to be static, to Joachim there was historical determinism that produced a fluid upward motion in man's affairs, always guided by God, and always present. His conception that time is divided into three parts is a dynamic of man's slow climb toward God after the Fall. It is a continuous process in which man and God strive to reunite in the last days. History has movement, regardless of temporal successes or failures. There is a destiny for man and the destiny is one of a better life in time on earth.

Judaism and Christianity, more than any of the other world religions, have always had high hopes for some golden age. St. Augustine pictured this golden age as the City of God, a model in a different dimension and time, but one to look toward and try to duplicate on earth. Joachim believed that change would occur as a part of the historical process begun with Adam. The implication was that change would occur as a result of Christian agencies at work in the world. Joachim of Fiore's influence upon later centuries is most important in its indirectness. His cosmic vision of history, ever moving forward toward a new age of peace and prosperity, was a seed for ideas of progress.

Joachim Studies:
The Current State of Affairs

J OACHIM OF FIORE remains a figure of considerable fascination to contemporary scholars and students of apocalypticism. Modern interest in the abbot's thought and influence has been spurred and guided by studies flowing primarily from the pens of European scholars, to name but a few: Herbert Grundmann, Ernst Benz, Ernesto Buonaiuti, Leone Tondelli, Henry Bett, Beatrice Hirsch-Reich, Antonio Crocco (Naples), Marjorie Reeves (St. Anne's College, Oxford), Cyprian Baraut (Abbey of Montserrat, Barcelona), and most recently, Gert Wendelborn (University of Rostock, East Germany) and Henry Mottu (Union Theological Seminary/Centre de Recontres de Cartigny, Geneva). In the last two decades, Americans have begun to take their place in scholarship on Joachim, and work on the abbot's literary corpus and its legacy has been and is being done by scholars such as Morton Bloomfield (Harvard University), Bernard McGinn (University of Chicago), and E. Randolph Daniel (University of Kentucky). Our intent in this brief bibliographic essay is to highlight some of the contributions made in the last decade of scholarly study to an understanding of the abbot's literary corpus and theology, and to indicate areas of concern which bear further investigation.

For a figure whose thought has captured as much interest as has Joachim's, editions of his works have been slow in appearing. Only minor works have found their way into modern print thus far: *Tractatus super Quatuor Evangelia* (1930), *De articulis fidei* and "Sermons" (1936), *Epistola universis Christi fidelibus* and *Epistola domini Valdonensi* (1937), *Dialogi de prescientia Dei et predestinatione electorum* (1938), *De titulo libri Apocalypsi* and *Enchiridion in Apocalypsim* (1938), *Hymnus de patria coelesti* (1899) and *Visio admiranda de gloria paradisi* (1899/1938), *De vita sancti Benedicti et de officio divino secundum ejus doctrinam* (1951), *Liber Figurarum* (1953), *Super flumina Babylonis*

(1953), *De septem sigillis* (1954), *Adversus Iudeos* (1957), "Testamentary Letter" (1960). Most recently, John V. Fleming and Marjorie Reeves have provided critical notes and a textual analysis with their modern edition of the *Hymnus* and *Visio*, under the title *Two Poems Attributed to Joachim of Fiore* (Pilgrim Press, 1980). Of these works, the edition of *De vita sancti Benedicti* stands most seriously in need of revision. Awaiting further study are the various introductions to Joachim's commentary on the Apocalypse, notably the *Enchiridion, De titulo libri Apocalypsi*, and the *Liber Introductorius* prefacing the Venetian edition of the *Expositio in Apocalypsim* (2v-26v). Critical editions need to be done, and their relationship to each other and to the *Expositio* itself needs to be determined.

Several of the minor works have been translated into English. Bernard McGinn has translated Joachim's "Testamentary Letter" and a substantial part of *De prophetia ignota*. He has also translated the texts of Table XIV of the *Liber Figurarum* ("The Seven-Headed Dragon"), and of Table XII ("The New People of God"), the *Epistola universis Christi fidelibus* ("Letter to All the Faithful"), and the *Epistola domini Valdonensi* ("Letter to the Abbot of Valdona"), the latter two based on the edition of J. Bignami-Odier with some minor corrections from the manuscript tradition.

The full texts of Joachim's three major commentaries, *Liber Concordie novi ac veteris Testamenti, Expositio in Apocalypsim*, and *Psalterium decem chordarum* are still accessible only through the Venetian editions of 1517 (*Liber Concordie*) and 1527 (*Expositio* and *Psalterium*), reprinted in 1964/65 by Minerva Press (Frankfurt/M). Long excerpts from these works were included by C. Hahn in his *Geschichte der Ketzer im Mittelalter* (1850), reprinted in 1968 by Scientia Verlag. In 1885, H. Denifle edited the findings of the Commission of Anagni, which included excerpts from these commentaries. Occasional differences between the texts quoted by the commission and the same texts in the Venetian editions witness to the often-noted unreliability of the latter. A further testimony to the problems encountered in the Venetian editions may be seen in the opening pages of the "Liber Primus" of the *Psalterium* which run in the following order: 228r/229r, 228v/229v, 231v/230v, 231/230r. Such problems are not insurmountable, however, nor are the editions unusable. Joachim's repetition of major ideas, symbols, and patterns allows for comparison of texts among the three commentaries and with the works for which a critical edition is available. A lengthy summary in English of the contents of the *Expositio in Apocalypsim* is provided in Vol. IV of E.B. Elliott's *Horae Apocalypticae* (Seeley, Jackson and Halliday, 1842), but there is no similar resource for either the *Liber Concordie* or the *Psalterium*.

The *Liber Concordie* stands as the most interesting of Joachim's commentaries, both in its organization and in its presentation of various historical schemata. Work on an edition of this major commentary is being done by E. Randolph Daniel. As the first fruits of his labors, he has provided a critical text of passages from Book II, Tract I, Chapter 8 in his article, "The Double Procession of the Holy Spirit in Joachim of Fiore's Understanding of History" (*Speculum*, 1980). In addition, he has translated Chapters 2 through 12 of this same book and tract. The availability of this section of the *Liber Concordie* in an English translation based on critical textual work is particularly fortuitous. First, Joachim's distinction between the exegetical principal of harmony (*concordia*) and that of allegory is most clearly stated and illustrated here. Second, the arguments for the three-epoch schema of history are presented and reveal the abbot's economic sense of the Trinity and history. Finally, the emendation of the text clarifies Joachim's understanding of the trinitarian doctrine of the double procession of the Spirit in its implications for the three-epoch schema of history.

While editorial work on Joachim's literary corpus has been somewhat sporadic, analyses of his thought and influence have kept a steady pace. Useful resources in the historiography of Joachim Studies have recently appeared. Delno West edited two volumes of previously published articles concerning the abbot of Fiore and his followers under the title of *Joachim of Fiore in Christian Thought*. The subtitle of the work, "Essays on the influence of the Calabrian Prophet," is particularly apt. With few exceptions, scholars have been primarily interested in showing the ways in which Joachim's apocalyptic ideas may have provided an impetus for other later figures and movements. The work begins with three articles which represent critical summaries of scholarship concerning the abbot of Fiore. The remaining seventeen articles concern the spread of Joachim's ideas, his influence on later religious orders, and his influence on church and state. These latter articles witness to the myriad directions which are taken by scholars in tracing Joachim's impact in the history of Christianity and Christian thought, and thus to the relative breadth of Joachim Studies.

Nineteenth- and twentieth-century interest in medieval apocalypticism in general, and in Joachim in particular, is succinctly chronicled by Bernard McGinn in two articles: "Apocalypticism in the Middle Ages: An Historiographical Sketch" (*Medieval Studies*, 1975), and "Awaiting an End: Research in Medieval Apocalypticism, 1974–1981" (*Medievalia et Humanistica*, 1982). The value of these articles goes beyond their brief review of some hundred and fifty years of scholarly reflections on medieval views of the end of history. McGinn discusses each scholar's work within the appropriate school of thought, and shows the connection between each particular interpretation of apocalypticism and the then-current methods of historical research. Perhaps McGinn's most important contribution here is to sketch the more recent lines of tradition in the interpretation of medieval apocalyptic thought.

The significance of the *Liber Figurarum* for an understanding of Joachim's thought and his subsequent influence has been the focus of much study by Marjorie Reeves. Together with Beatrice Hirsch-Reich, the English scholar argued in *The Figurae of Joachim of Fiore* that the *Liber Figurarum* was one of the abbot's genuine works, genuine here meaning done either by the abbot himself or directly under his supervision. Although the authors have not demonstrated Joachim's authorship of the *Liber Figurarum* to everyone's satisfaction, they have shown that this collection of figures has a contribution to make in understanding Joachim's ideas. In establishing a relationship between the figures of the *Liber Figurarum* and Joachim's commentaries, Reeves and Hirsch-Reich also established that the visualization of symbols "in the mind's eye" was an integral part of Joachim's modus operandi. The abbot organized and expressed his thoughts through symbols drawn from the Bible and the Fathers. The figures of the *Liber Figurarum* serve to highlight the various symbolic patterns set forth in Joachim's writings and to emphasize the complexity of his ideas, especially those concerning history. As Reeves and Hirsch-Reich point out, the figures (e.g., "The New People of God") integrate several symbolic patterns found scattered throughout Joachim's commentaries. Because of occasional differences in detail between the figures and the texts of the commentaries, the two scholars argue that in many cases the figures represent a final clarification of the abbot's ideas.

The question of the authorship of the *Liber Figurarum* remains intriguing. Bernard McGinn offers the interesting suggestion that the immediate disciples were compilers and editors. He states that those figures which Joachim himself apparently drew and captioned were, after his death, collected and edited by his disciples into the *Liber Figurarum*. McGinn's reconstruction lends credence to the way in which the *Liber Figurarum* has generally been handled. Individual figures have been analyzed in relation to the ideas set forth in Joachim's commentaries and have been used to emphasize certain aspects of those ideas, for example, the tree figures have been used to illustrate the organic nature of Joachim's view of history. As a work which may have its own integrity, the *Liber Figurarum* has been examined primarily as a vehicle for the spread of Joachim's ideas.

The *Liber Figurarum* was not the only form in which the abbot of Fiore's ideas were circulated after his death. Especially through short tracts such as *De septem sigillis* and *Epistola universis Christi fidelibus* and figures such as the Table of Concords (parallels between the Old and New Testament histories), Joachim's thought was represented in collections which Reeves has termed "prophetic anthologies." In Appendix C of *The Influence of Prophecy in the Later Middle Ages* (Clarendon Press, 1969), Reeves has analyzed the contents of some of these anthologies. The prophetic anthologies vary widely in what they include, some containing only genuine and pseudo-Joachite works, others combining the genuine and pseudo-Joachite works with other popular prophetic forms such as the Sibylline oracles; Reeves does not analyze any anthologies devoid of Joachite influence. Reeves' work on the literary corpus of Joachim and those coming under his influence is a contribution to the study of the literary genres important in medieval apocalypticism. This analysis of literature also provides much of the evidence on which Reeves bases her study of Joachimism in the later Middle Ages. Tracing that history through the Renaissance and Reformation is the focus of *Joachim and the Prophetic Future* (SPCK, 1976). Both *The Influence of Prophecy in the Later Middle Ages* and *Joachim and the Prophetic Future* bring form and organization to such a detailed and complex subject as Joachim's influence; both books remain starting points for the study of Joachimism. With the publication of *Prophecy and Millenarianism: Essays in Honor of Marjorie Reeves* (Longman, 1980), the English scholar's preeminence in the field of scholarship on apocalypticism has been acknowledged.

Analyses of Joachim's understanding of history have been done primarily out of an interest in the abbot's contributions to the history of thought, in particular to theology and philosophy of history. For many years the discussion has focused on whether Joachim's idea of a third epoch gives rise to a view of history as progress. Studies in the last decade have tended to acknowledge the complexity of the abbot's understanding of history and to examine that understanding as an example of medieval apocalyptic thought. These studies have shared the goals of overcoming for the modern reader the strangeness of Joachim's logic and of appreciating Joachim's method of inquiry as an example of the medieval symbolic mentality at work. For modern scholars, Joachim's writings provide a fruitful ground for examining the relationships between a method of interpretation (hermeneutics) and the kind of knowledge that can be gleaned from the historical process.

Based on his own very extensive study for an unpublished Jena *Habilitationschrift*, Gert Wendelborn has provided an analysis of Joachim's theology of history in *Gott und Geschichte* (Böhlaus, 1974). The interest conveyed by the title of Wendelborn's dissertation, "Theology of History and Hermeneutics in the Work of Joachim of Fiore," carries over into this published volume. For Wendelborn, Joachim's allegorical method of interpreting Scripture does not lead to a realm of eternal truth, but rather is used to establish the ideals of each historical epoch. The German scholar argues that Joachim could only understand history as a history of salvation in which the "truths of faith" are most relevant because they are part of the historical reality itself. According to Wendelborn, Joachim's third epoch represents a radical breakthrough of the ecclesiastical forms of the second epoch by the dynamic of the Spirit. He asserts that Joachim's understanding of history is one of progress, more radical than the abbot himself could have admitted. But Wendelborn acknowledges the complexity of Joachim's historical schemata. He argues, finally, that the identification and understanding of such repetitive patterns in history encourages responsible participation in the historical process.

In *La manifestation de l'Esprit selon Joachim de Fiore* (Delachaux & Niestle, 1977), Henry Mottu provides a detailed examination of Joachim's *Tractatus super Quatuor Evangelia*. Mottu finds this last-written commentary of the abbot the most radical of his works and a useful focus for studying the interface between symbol and history, mysticism and apocalypticism. Indeed, Mottu includes among his motivations for studying

Joachim's thought a desire to show the relationship between hermeneutics and prophecy, and a desire to rehabilitate the role of apocalypticism in theology and the history of doctrine. What makes Mottu's analysis particularly interesting is that he seeks to apply to Joachim's interpretation of biblical figures and events the insights into symbolism provided by phenomenologists such as Paul Ricoeur. Mottu's work may contribute as much to the science of method as to an understanding of the abbot himself. In Mottu's estimation, Joachim's contribution was an appreciation of the fundamental historicity of the human being, the need to be situated in a particular temporal context, awaiting the coming of the Heavenly City.

The need to discern the relationship between time and eternity, between the historicity of human life and the heavenly realm, is a central concern of apocalypticism, according to Bernard McGinn. The University of Chicago scholar considers that the description and definition of apocalypticism has been too long the domain of biblical scholars. He argues that apocalypticism did not die out in the second century but has remained a continuing part of the Christian tradition. While the literary genre of the Apocalypse was abandoned, the need to express expectations of the imminent end found outlets in other forms, for example, in the commentary, a text upon a text. In two books, *Visions of the End* (Columbia University Press, 1979) and *Apocalyptic Spirituality* (Paulist Press, 1979), McGinn has collected and translated numerous apocalyptic texts ranging from 400 to 1500 A.D. The contribution of these volumes to an understanding of Joachim's thought may be assessed on two levels: the selection of the texts from Joachim's writings and their place within the larger collection.

Visions of the End is the more extensive of the two works, containing short selections from more than thirty-five authors. In his selection of texts, McGinn has been guided by a concern to represent classic statements on topics reflecting the interests of patristic and medieval apocalypticism. He includes nine selections from Joachim, drawn from the *Expositio in Apocalypsim, De prophetia ignota, Liber Concordie, Quatuor Evangelia*, and *Liber Figurarum*. The selections cover a range of topics, including Joachim's revelation concerning the harmony between the Old and New Testaments, the three epochs, the Antichrist, and the papacy. These topics are certainly concerns of the abbot of Fiore and a good representation of his positions. Yet with the exception of the lengthy section from the *De prophetia ignota*, the texts present primarily Joachim's conclusions and very little of his mode of argumentation. In the context

119

of this selection of apocalyptic writings, however, the selections from Joachim's writings work well to convey a sense of where Joachim's opinion on one of these topics, for example, his picture of the Antichrist, is to be located in the Christian apocalyptic tradition.

Apocalyptic Spirituality is narrower in scope, containing selections from only six authors: Lactantius, Adso of Montier-en-Der, Joachim of Fiore, Angelo of Clareno, Peter John Olivi, and Savonarola. McGinn's selection of texts here has been guided by a desire to show how each author's expectations about the end of history govern his presentation of and admonitions for life in the present. The selections from Joachim are the "Letter to All the Faithful," "Letter to the Abbot of Valdona," *Liber Concordie*, Book I, Part I, Chapters 2–12 (translated by E. Randolph Daniel), "The Seven-Headed Dragon," and "The New People of God." The importance of the text from the *Liber Concordie* for understanding Joachim's method of interpretation and his theology of history has been noted above. The texts of the two letters provide examples of the ways in which Joachim approached a general audience with his concerns and expectations for the present and the future. Finally, the texts that accompany the two figures from the *Liber Figurarum* convey two of the abbot's more interesting ideas: a schema of the last things based on the figure of the red dragon with seven heads and ten horns (Apoc. 12:3–4), and the monastery plan which envisions life in the third epoch. As selections of texts to convey the abbot's mode of thought and to provide a balanced perspective on his concerns, the selections in *Apocalyptic Spirituality* are far superior to those in *Visions of the End*. As an aid in determining Joachim's place in the history of apocalyptic thought, however, this group of texts is less helpful.

While Joachim's influence on the subsequent tradition of apocalyptic thought has been extensively studied, his relation to the patristic tradition remains ambiguous. We have tried to compare Joachim's views of history to those of St. Augustine, for example, in Chapter III of this book, but the precise nature of the abbot of Fiore's dependence on the church fathers has yet to be thoroughly examined. Most often Joachim is seen as breaking with the previous tradition. One scholar to challenge this view is Robert Lerner (Northwestern University). In "Refreshment of the Saints" (*Traditio*, 1976), Lerner focuses on the idea of an intervening time between Antichrist and Last Judgment, finding the genesis of such a notion in St. Jerome's commentary on Daniel. He traces the development of the idea from St. Jerome through the early Reformation, concluding that the twelfth century marked a turning point in the elaboration of the idea and that Joachim gave the most imaginative presentation of it in his concept of a third epoch. The innovation usually accorded to Joachim's third epoch must therefore be modified by the fact that he is elaborating on an idea which has its roots in the tradition of the orthodox fathers.

Defining more precisely the relationship of Joachim to the patristic and early medieval periods, especially in the matter of the abbot's sources, is one of the important areas of research to be undertaken in the next decade. A major aid in this endeavor will be the publication in the near future of E. Randolph Daniel's edition of the *Liber Concordie*. The *Expositio* and *Psalterium* await critical editions, while textual work on the shorter tracts should continue. Study of the abbot's method of interpretation has not been exhausted, especially in the area of the organization and structure which Joachim brings to his commentaries. With the current widespread interest in hermeneutics, it is likely that this will continue to be a subject of investigation. The relation between Joachim's peculiar ideas of history and the perhaps less distinctive aspects of his theology revealed in tracts like the *De articulis fidei* and in sermons and letters should be examined. Joachim was, after all, not only a prophet and theologian of history, but also an abbot, a spiritual teacher.

Selected Bibliography

Books

Benz, Ernst. *Ecclesia spiritualis*. Stuttgart: Kohlhammer, 1934.

Bett, H. *Joachim of Flora*. London: Methuen, 1931. Reprint edition, Merrik, New York: Richwood Publishing Company, 1976.

Buonaiuti, E. *Gioacchino da Fiore*. Rome: Collezione meridionale editrice, 1931.

Crocco, Antonio. *Gioacchino da Fiore*. Naples: Auria, 1960.

Daniel, E. Randolph. *The Franciscan Concept of Mission in the High Middle Ages*. Lexington: The University of Kentucky Press, 1975.

Fleming, John V., and Marjorie Reeves, editors. *Two Poems Attributed to Joachim of Fiore*. Princeton: Pilgrim Press, 1978.

Grundmann, Herbert. *Neue Forschungen über Joachim von Fiore*. Marburg: Simons, 1950.

_____. *Studien über Joachim von Floris*. Leipzig: Teubner, 1927. Reprint edition, Darmstadt: W.B., 1966.

McGinn, Bernard. *Visions of the End*. New York: Columbia University Press, 1979.

Mottu, Henry. *La manifestation de l'Esprit selon Joachim de Fiore*. Neuchatal and Paris: Delachaux & Niestle, 1977.

Ratzinger, Joseph. *The Theology of History of St. Bonaventure*. Translated by Z. Hayes. Chicago: Franciscan Herald Press, 1971.

Reeves, Marjorie. *Joachim of Fiore and the Prophetic Future*. London: SPCK, 1976.

_____. *Prophecy in the Later Middle Ages*. Oxford: Clarendon Press, 1969.

Reeves, Marjorie, and Beatrice Hirsch-Reich. *The Figurae of Joachim of Fiore*. Oxford: Clarendon Press, 1972.

Wendelborn, Gert. *Gott und Geschichte*. Vienna: Hermann Bohlaus, 1974.

West, Delno, editor. *Joachim of Fiore in Christian Thought*. Two volumes. New York: Burt Franklin, 1975.

Selected Articles and Monographs
Joachim's Thought and Influence

Baraut, Cipriano. "Joachim de Flore." *Dictionnaire de spiritualité*, 8:1179–1201.

Bischoff, Guntram. "Early Premonstratensian Eschatology: The Apocalyptic Myth." In *The Spirituality of Western Christendom*, pp. 41–71. Edited by E. Rozanne Elder. Kalamazoo, Michigan: Cistercian Publication, 1976.

Bloomfield, Morton W. "Joachim of Flora: A Critical Survey of his Canon,

122

Teaching, Sources, Biography, and Influence." *Traditio* (1957), 13:249–311.

Funkenstein, Amos. "Periodization and Self-Understanding in the Middle Ages and Early Modern Times." *Medievalia et Humanistica: Studies in Medieval and Renaissance Culture.* New Series, No. 5: Medieval Historiography, pp. 3–24. Edited by Paul Maurice Clogan. Denton, Texas: North Texas State University, 1974.

Grundmann, Herbert. "Zur Biographie Joachims von Fiore und Raniers von Ponza." *Deutsches Archiv für Erforschung des Mittelalters* (1960), 16:437–546.

Leff, Gordon. "The Making of the Myth of a True Church in the Later Middle Ages." *Journal of Medieval and Renaissance Studies* (1971), 1:1–16.

Lerner, Robert E. "Joachim of Fiore as a Link between St. Bernard and Innocent III on the Figural Significance of Melchisedech." *Mediaeval Studies* (1980), 42:471–476.

_____. "Refreshment of the Saints: The Time After Antichrist as a Station for Earthly Progress in Medieval Thought." *Traditio* (1976), 32:97–144.

Lubac, Henri de. *Exégèse médiévale: Les quatre sens de l'Écriture.* Vol. 1, pt. 2:437–558. Paris: Aubier, 1961.

McGinn, Bernard. "Apocalypticism in the Middle Ages: An Historiographical Sketch." *Mediaeval Studies* (1975), 37:252–286.

_____. "Awaiting an End: Research in Medieval Apocalypticism, 1974–1981." *Medievalia et Humanistica: Studies in Medieval and Renaissance Culture.* New Series, No. 11, pp. 263–289. Edited by Paul Maurice Clogan. Totowa, N.J.: Rowman and Littlefield, 1982.

_____. "Joachim and the Sibyl." *Cîteaux* (1973), 2:97–138.

Pickering, F. "Irrwege der mittelalterlichen Geschichtsschreibung (Rupert von Deutz, Joachim von Fiore)." *Zeitschrift für deutsches Alterum und deutsche Literatur* (1971), 100:270–296.

Reeves, Marjorie. "The Abbot Joachim's Sense of History." *Colloques internationaux du centre national de la recherche scientifique* (1977), 558:781–796. Paris, Editions du centre national de la recherche scientifique, 1977.

_____. "History and Prophecy in Medieval Thought." *Medievalia et Humanistica: Studies in Medieval and Renaissance Culture.* New Series, no. 5: Medieval Historiography, pp. 51–76. Edited by Paul Maurice Clogan. Denton, Texas: North Texas State University, 1974.

Reeves, Marjorie, and Beatrice Hirsch-Reich. "The Seven Seals in the Writings of Joachim of Fiore." *Recherches de théologie ancienne et médiévale* (1954), 21:211–247.

Sandrail, M. "Joachim de Flore, le messager des derniers temps." *Bulletin de l'Association Guillaume Budé* (1970), 3/iv:407–424.

Wendelborn, Gert. "Die Hermeneutik des kalabreisischen Abtes Joachim von Fiore." *Communio Viatorum* (1974), 17:63–91.

Williams, Ann. Editor. *Prophecy and Millenarianism: Essays in Honour of Marjorie Reeves.* London: Longman's Press, 1980.

Zimdars-Swartz, Sandra. "The Fifth Order of Fire: The Significance of the Exegetical Plan of Joachim of Fiore's Four Major Commentaries." Unpublished doctoral dissertation. Claremont Graduate School, 1978.

Selected Bibliography

_____. "Joachim of Flore." *Dictionnaire des auteurs cisterciens.* 16/ii:419–423. Abbaye Notre-Dame de St-Remy, Belgium: La documentation cistercienne, 1977.

_____. "Joachim of Fiore and the Cistercian Order: A Study of *De vita sancti Benedicti.*" *Studies in Medieval Cistercian History,* IV: Simplicity and Ordinariness, pp. 293–309. Edted by John Sommerfeldt. Kalamazoo, Michigan: Cistercian Publications, 1980.

_____. "The Trinity and History: An Introduction to Twelfth-Century Theology of History." *Religion Journal of Kansas* (1979), 17/i: 1–6.

Selected Articles and Monographs
Joachites and Joachimism

Bignami-Odier, Jeanne. *Études sur Jean de Roquetaillade.* Paris: Vrin, 1952.

Bloomfield, Morton, and Marjorie Reeves. "The Penetration of Joachimism into Northern Europe." *Speculum* (1954), 29:772–793.

Burr, David. "The Apocalyptic Element in Olivi's Critique of Aristotle." *Church History* (1971), 40:15–29.

_____. *The Persecution of Peter Olivi.* Transactions of the American Philosophical Society, 66, Philadelphia, 1976.

_____. "Petrus Ioannis Olivi and the Philosophers." *Franciscan Studies* (1971), 31:41–71.

Daniel, E. Randolph. "Apocalyptic Conversion: The Joachite Alternative to the Crusades." *Traditio* (1969), 25:127–154.

_____. "A Re-examination of the Origins of Franciscan Joachitism." *Speculum* (1968), 43:371–676.

_____. "Roger Bacon and the *De Seminibus Scripturarum.*" *Mediaeval Studies* (1972), 34:462–467.

_____. "Spirituality and Poverty: Angelo da Clareno and Ubertino da Casale." *Medievalia et Humanistica.* New Series, No. 4: Medieval and Renaissance Spirituality, pp. 89–98. Edited by Paul Maurice Clogan. 1973.

Davis, Charles, "Le Pape Jean XXII et les spirituels: Ubertin de Casale." *Franciscains d'Oc.* Cahiers de Fanjeaux, 10. Toulouse: Privat, 1975.

Lee, Harold. "Scrutamini Scripturas: Joachimist Themes and Figurae in the Early Religious Writings of Arnold of Villanova." *Journal of the Warburg and Courtauld Institutes* (1974), 37:33–56.

Lerner, Robert. "Medieval Prophecy and Religious Dissent." *Past and Present* (1976), 72:3–24.

Lowith, Karl. *Meaning in History.* Chicago: University of Chicago Press, 1949.

Manselli, Raoul. *La Lectura super Apocalypsim di Pietro di Giovanni Olivi: Recherche sull'escatologismo medioevale.* Istituto Storico Italiano per il Medio Evo. Studi Storici, 19–21. Rome: Sede dell'Istituto, 1955.

_____. "Spirituali e Beguini in Provenza." *Istituto Storico Italiano per il Medio Evo, Studi Storici,* 31–34. Rome: Sede dell'Istituto, 1959.

McGinn, Bernard. "Angel Pope and Papal Antichrist." *Church History* (1978), 47:155–173.

_____. "The Significance of Bonaventure's Theology of History." Celebrating the Medieval Heritage. *Journal of Religion Supplement,* David Tracy, ed. (1978), 58:64–81.

Messini, A. "Profitismo e profezie ritmiche italiana d'ispirazione Gioachimito-Francescana nei secoli XII, XIV e XV." *Miscellanea Francescana* (1937), 37:39–54.

Partee, Carter. "Peter John Olivi: Historical and Doctrinal Study." *Franciscan Studies* (1960), 20:215–260.

Phalen, John. *The Millennial Kingdom of the Franciscans in the New World.* Berkeley and Los Angeles: University of California Press, 1970.

Ratzinger, Joseph. *The Theology of History in St. Bonaventure.* trans. by Z. Hayes. Chicago: Franciscan Herald Press, 1971.

Reeves, Marjorie. "The Abbot Joachim's Disciples and the Cistercian Order." *Sophia* (1951), 19:355–371.

_____. "Some Popular Prophecies from the Fourteenth to the Seventeenth Centuries." *Studies in Church History*, 8. In *Popular Belief and Practice*, ed. by G. Cuming and D. Baker. Cambridge: At the University Press, 1972.

_____. "History and Eschatology: Medieval and Early Protestant Thought in Some English and Scottish Writings." *Medievalia et Humanistica: Studies in Medieval and Renaissance Culture.* New Series, no. 4: Medieval and Renaissance Spirituality, pp. 99–123. Edited by Paul Maurice Clogan. 1973.

Simoni, Fiorella. "Il super Hieremiam e il Gioachimismo Francescano." *Bollettino dell'Istituto Storico Italiano per il Medio Evo* (1970), 82:13–46.

West, Delno. "Between Flesh and Spirit: Joachite Themes in the Cronica of Fra Salimbene." *The Journal of Medieval History* (1977), 3:339–352.

_____. "The Reformed Church and the Friars Minor: The Moderate Joachite Position of Fra Salimbene." *Archivum Franciscanum Historicum* (1971), 64:273–284.

_____. "A Note on the Date of the Expositio super Regulam of Hugh of Digne." *Journal of the Rocky Mountain Medieval and Renaissance Association* (1980), 1:75–78.

Notes

Introduction

1. Beside the great commentators on the Apocalypse, the early Middle Ages abound with sculpture, painting, stained glass, manuscript illuminations, and mosaics inspired by St. John's vision, see M. Vloberg, "The Bible as Art," *Guide to the Bible* (Paris-Tournae, 1955) II, pp. 547ff., and W. Neuss, *Die Apokalypse de hl. Jonnes in der altspanischen und Altchristlicher Bibel-Illustration* (Munster, 1931).

2. E. Buonaiuti, *Gioacchino da Fiore, i tempi, la vita, il messaggio* (Rome, 1931), p. 8.

3. M. Reeves and R. Hirsch-Reich, *The Figurae of Joachim of Fiore* (Oxford, 1972), pp. 21, 95, 255–256.

Chapter I

1. For a complete list of biographical sources and a comparative analysis of them, see H. Grundmann, "Zur Biographie Joachims von Fiore and Raiers von Ponza," *Deutsches Archiv für Enforschung des Mittelalters*, 16 (1960), pp. 539–544.

2. EA, 39r.

3. Luke of Cosenza, "Virtutum Beati Joachimi synopsis," in H. Grundmann, "Zur Biographie . . . ," p. 504.

4. Salimbene de Adam, *Cronica*, ed. O. Holder-Egger (Monumenta Germaniae Historica, XXXII, Hanover and Leipzig, 1913), p. 241.

5. EA, 81v.

6. B. Jaffe, *Regesta Pontificum Romanorum*, II (Graz, 1956) no. 17425.

7. The text of his sermon which was an explanation of a sybillian oracle is contained in the *De prophetia ignota*, edited by B. McGinn, "Joachim and the Sibyl," *Citeaux*, no. 2 (1973), pp. 129–138.

8. Salimbene, *Cronica*, p. 457. A fuller discussion of this scandal is found on pp. 104–105.

9. F. Manuel, *Shapes of Philosophical History* (Stanford, 1965), p. 36.

Chapter II

1. See, F. Burkitt, *The Book of Rules of Tyconius* (Text and Studies: Contributions to Biblical and Patristic Literature, III, no. 1, Cambridge, 1894).

2. LC 111; EA 106.

3. EA 39r.

4. Reeves and Hirsch-Reich, *Figurae*, p. 5.

5. LC 18r; EA 9–10, 115r.

6. V. Hopper, *Medieval Number Symbolism* (New York, 1938), p. 99.

7. Augustine of Hippo, *City of God* (in *Nicene and Post Nicene Fathers of the Church*, II, ed. M. Dods), v. 21.

8. LC 112r.

9. EA 5v.

10. EA 5.

11. EA 6–10.

12. Reeves and Hirsch-Reich, *Figurae*, p. 13.

13. The Joachites devoted a separate treatise to explaining the Seven Seals, *De septem sigillis*, in relation to his grand scheme. For an analysis of this treatise and others, see M. Reeves and B. Hirsch-Reich, "The Seven Seals in the writings of Joachim of Fiore," *Recherches de théologie ancienne et médiévale*, 21 (1954), pp. 211–247.

14. Other discussions of the seven seals occur in LC, book 3, and in the "Liber Introductorius" which precedes EA.

15. EA 210v.

16. LC 71r.

17. LC 112v.

Chapter III

1. EA 19v, 71r, 110v; John Chrysostom is added to the list in LC 46r, LC 66v.

2. Buonaiuti considers *On the Predestination of the Saints*, 19, to be the source for a quotation which Joachim identifies as belonging to St. Augustine, although the text Buonaiuti cites does not match that quoted by Joachim. DAF 34:3–4, and note 1.

3. E. Randolph Daniel takes Joachim's use of the term "Moechus" to be based on the notion that this was the name of the father of Romulus and Remus. *Apocalyptic Spirituality*, ed. B. McGinn (New York: Paulist Press, 1979), "Section C: The Book of Concordance," p. 293, note 20.

4. The text of this figure is translated by B. McGinn in *Apocalyptic Spirituality*, pp. 136–141.

5. For Joachim's discussion of *concordia*, see LC 7r-8r; for his recounting of the experience in which the harmony between the Old and New Testaments was revealed to him, see EA 39r-v.

6. LC, Books II, III and IV; see also Chapter II.

7. Joachim's information here is taken from Eusebius, *History of the Church*, G. A. Williamson, trans. (Baltimore: Penguin, 1965), II:17.

8. C. Baraut, "Un Tratado Inedito de Joaquin de Fiore," *Analecta sacra Tarraconensia* 24 (1951), p. 35. Joachim comments at length on Chapters 8, 9, and 11 of the Rule, and briefly on Chapters 10, 12, 13, 15, and 17.

9. S. Zimdars-Swartz, "Joachim of Fiore and the Cistercian Order: A Study of *De vita sancti Benedicti*," *Studies in Medieval Cistercian History IV: Simplicity and Ordnariness*, ed. J. Sommerfeldt (Kalamazoo, Michigan: Cistercian Publications, 1980), pp. 293–309.

10. See also discussion of the *Rotae* in Reeves and Hirsch-Reich, *Figurae*, pp. 224–231. Joachim's indebtedness to Pope Gregory and St. Jerome is noted on p. 226, note 9.

11. For texts illustrating Pope Gregory's apocalypticism, see B. McGinn, *Visions of the End: Apocalyptic Traditions in the Middle Ages* (New York: Columbia University Press, 1979), pp. 62–65.

12. For the identification of Remigius as Haimo of Auxerre, see R. Lerner, "Refreshment of the Saints: The Time after Antichrist as a Station for Earthly Progress in Medieval Thought," *Traditio* 32 (1976), p. 117 and note 63.

13. M. Reeves, *Joachim of Fiore and the Prophetic Future* (London: SPCK, 1976), pp. 176–177 and note 6.

14. For the most recent comparisons, see M. Reeves, "History and Prophecy in Medieval Thought," *Medievalia et Humanistica*, no. 5 (1974), pp. 54–55; and S. Zimdars-Swartz, "The Trinity and History: An Introduction to Twelfth-Century Theology of History," *Religion Journal of Kansas* (October, 1979), pp. 1–6.

15. Gaston Salet, ed., *Anselm de Havelberg: Dialogi*, Sources chretiennes, no. 118 (Paris: Cerf, 1966), pp. 26–118.

16. Anselm's five periods of Old Testament history are Adam to Noah, Noah to Abraham, Abraham to Moses, Moses to David, David to Christ.

17. Jean Gribomont, "Introduction" to *Rupert de Deutz: Les oeuvres du Saint-Esprit*, Sources chretiennes, no. 131 (Paris: Cert, 1967), pp. 8–12.

18. *De Trinitate et operibus ejus* constitutes the first volume of Rupert's works in the *Patrologia cursus completus, series Latina* (PL), Vol. 167. A translation of part of the Preface is found in McGinn, *Visions of the End*, p. 110.

Chapter IV

1. LC, Preface, 5v, 43v–44r; EA 3v.

2. Joachim does not define these terms precisely. His most concise theological statement of the content of these secrets and mysteries would be "the deep counsels, hidden from the ancient days and generations of the world" (*alta concilia abscondita a diebus antiquis et a generationibus seculorum*. I Cor. 2:7).

3. LC, Preface, 5v; STA, p. 289; EA 3v.

4. Joachim has long been known to be indebted to St. Paul for his distinction between "the latter which kills and the spirit which makes alive" (I Cor. 3:6). Reeves and Hirsch-Reich, *Figurae*, p. 3, notes 16 and 17, have noted this indebtedness; and G. Wendelborn has catalogued other citations which Joachim drew from the Pauline letters in "Die Hermeneutik des kalabresischen Abtes Joachim von Fiore," *Communio Viatorum* 17 (1974), pp. 86–87.

5. The best general discussions of Joachim's methods for the interpretation of Scripture are H. de Lubac, *Exégèse médiévale: Les quatres sens de l'Écriture*, I (Paris, 1959–1964), pp. 437–558; and Wendelborn, "Die Hermeneutik . . . ," pp. 63–91.

6. Reeves, "History and Prophecy in Medieval Thought," pp. 57–59.

7. Joachim uses interchangeably the designations "Order of Married" and "Order of Laity."

8. A. Crocco has done the initial work in showing the influence of the

Latin fathers on Joachim's trinitarian doctrine in *Gioacchino da Fiore* (Naples: M. D'Auria, 1960), pp. 109–111; "La formatione doctrinale de Gioacchino da Fiore e le fonti delle sua teologia trinitaria," *Sophia* 25 (1955), pp. 192–196; and "La teologia trinitaria de Gioacchino da Fiore," *Sophia* 25 (1957), pp. 218–232.

9. Joachim makes frequent reference to these five relationships and some variations on them: PDC 257v, 260r–262r; EA 38r; LC 61v.

10. For comments on Joachim's understanding of scholastic theology, see B. McGinn, "The Abbott and the Doctors: Scholastic Reactions to the Radical Eschatology of Joachim of Fiore," *Church History* 40 (1971), pp. 454–455.

11. *Licet ergo tres persone secundum substantiam dicantur, licet essentia personarum secundum substantiam dicatur. Hoc tamen interest quod nomen persone prolatum in plurali numero pluralitatem indicat, singularitatem devitat et nomen substantie unitatem retinet nihil scissionis aut divisions admittens.* PDC 232r.

12. For a discussion of the versions of the Psaltery in the *figurae*, see Reeves and Hirsch-Reich, *Figurae*, pp. 199–211.

13. E.R. Daniel has examined Joachim's arguments for the three-epoch (*status*) schema and its relation to the two-Dispensation schema in "The Double Procession of the Holy Spirit in Joachim of Fiore's Understanding of History," *Speculum* 55 (1980), pp. 469–483. Daniel has translated Book II, Tract I, Chapters 2–12 of the *Liber Concordie* in *Apocalyptic Spirituality*, pp. 120–134.

14. The Venetian text of this passage (LC 9v) is inaccurate. For a critical edition of the passage and the implications of the variant reading for Joachim's understanding of the theology of history, see "The Double Procession of the Holy Spirit . . . , pp. 472–473.

15. See also, PDC 259r-260r for a discussion of five times based on the five possible relations of the Trinity to each other and to creatures; here the five times are before the law, under the law, under the kings and prophets, under the Son and Holy Spirit, under the Holy Spirit. Joachim does not relate this discussion to the three epochs.

16. For a full discussion of the times of each state, see M. Reeves "The Abbot Joachim's Sense of History," *Colloques internationaux du centre national de la recherche scientifique*, 558 (1977), pp. 790–795.

17. DAF, pp. 42–44. In the *Dialogi de praescientia Dei et praedestinatione electorum* (p. 283), Joachim goes so far as to state: "Therefore the reason for election is not righteousness, but abjection, not the consolation of the world, but affliction, not because these things simply please God, but because they bring forth humility, which is the only virtue God requires in angels and men." (*Igitur electonis causa non iustitia est, sed abiectio, non consolatio mundi, sed afflictio, non quia ista simpliciter placent deo, sed quia pariunt humilitatem quam solam requirit virtutem deus in angelis et hominibus.*)

18. LC 17v, 20v, 39v, 44r-v.

19. LC 20v; TSQE, pp. 139, 178, 219–221, 222.

20. LC 70v-71r, 115r, 117r, 126r, 133r; TSQE, pp. 24, 101, 150, 195, 229, 143; STA, p. 296; EA 24r-v, 146r-148v, 166v-167r, 203v, 209r, 213v.

21. LC 69v-70r; STA, p. 299; Table XII of the *Liber Figurarum*.

Chapter V

1. The major discussions of the place of Christ in Joachim's theology of history are M. Reeves, *The Influence of Prophecy in the Later Middle Ages* (Oxford: Clarendon Press, 1969), pp. 126–132; and H. Mottu, *La manifestatione de l'Esprit selon Joachim de Fiore* (Paris: Delachaux & Niestle, 1977), pp. 321–328.

2. For remarks concerning the sending of the Son and Spirit in Joachim's trinitarian doctrine, see Crocce, "La Teologia trinitaria . . ." pp. 228–230; and McGinn, "The Abbot and the Doctors . . . ," pp. 254–255.

3. For a discussion on the variations in the labeling of the strings and the significance of these variations, see Reeves and Hirsch-Reich, *Figurae*, pp. 201–207.

4. See also the discussion of these two virtues in the *Psalterium* 241r.

5. E.R. Daniel has noted the importance of this scriptural passage for Joachim's understanding of the mission of the Holy Spirit. "The Double Procession of the Holy Spirit . . . ," pp. 479–480.

6. Reeves and Hirsch-Reich, *Figurae*, pp. 225–226.

Chapter VI

1. Daniel, "The Double Procession of the Holy Spirit . . . ," pp. 469–483 has shown the difficulty in grasping Joachim's historical meaning.

2. Reeves, *Influence of Prophecy*, pp. 518–533, for listings and locations of the many pseudo-Joachite manuscripts.

3. The primary study of the *Liber Figurarum*, of course, is Reeves and Hirsch-Reich, *Figurae*.

4. *Ibid.*, pp. 20ff.

5. M. Bloomfield and M. Reeves, "The Penetration of Joachimism into Northern Europe," *Speculum*, 29 (1954), pp. 772–793.

6. Salimbene, *Cronica*, pp. 236–237.

7. Bloomfield and Reeves, "Penetration of Joachimism . . . ," pp. 115–116.

8. Not only did Churchmen study his literature, but laymen were also attracted to him. Salimbene, for example, records for us a Joachite discussion group of doctors, lawyers, notaries, and other lettered men who regularly met with Hugh of Digne at his hermitage near Aix-en-Provence. *Cronica*, p. 236.

9. A detailed account of these events as well as surviving documents relating to the case may be found in H. Denifle, "Das Evangelium aeternum und die Commission zu Anagni," *Archiv für Literatur und Kirchengeschichte des Mittelalters* (Paris, 1885) I, pp. 49–142.

10. Daniel, "The Double Procession of the Holy Spirit . . . ," p. 479.

11. For an introduction to this problem, see E. Donckel, "Studien über die Prophezeiung des Fr. Telephorus von Cosenza, O.F.M.," *Archivum Franciscanum Historicum*, 26 (1933), pp. 29–104 and 282–314. A recent treatment of the subject is Reeves, *Joachim of Fiore and the Prophetic Future*, pp. 59–83.

12. LC 59v.

13. D. West, "The Reformed Church and the Friars Minor: The Mod-

erate Joachite Position of Fra Salimbene," *Archivum Franciscanum Historicum*, 64 (1971), pp. 276–277.

14. C. Lyttle, "The Stigmata of St. Francis Considered in Light of Possible Joachimite Influences upon Thomas of Celano," *Papers of the American Society of Church History*, IV, ser. 2 (1914), p. 83.

15. For a complete study of this investigation, see D. Burr, *The Persecution of Peter Olivi* (Transactions of the American Philosophical Society, 66. Philadelphia, 1976).

16. John Wycliff, *The Last Age of the Church*, ed. J. Todd (Dublin, 1840), pp. xxiv, lii, liii.

17. John Bale, *A Brief Chronycle Concernynge the Examynacyon and Death of the Blessed Martyr of Christ, Sir John Oldcastell, the Lorde Cobham* (London, 1729).

18. *Ibid.*, pp. 111–112.

19. In *Select Works of John Bale*, H. Christmas, ed. (Cambridge, 1849).

20. Nicholas Bernard, *Certain Discourses, Viz. of Babylon (Rev. 18:4) Being the Present See of Rome* (London, 1659), pp. 118–125.

21. Edward Bickersteth, *A Practical Guide to the Prophecies* (London, 1836), p. 171.

22. J. Phelan, *The Millennial Kingdom of the Franciscans in the New World* (Berkeley and Los Angeles, 1970), pp. 135–136 and notes 25, 26, 27, 28.

23. Phelan suggests that this "prophecy" actually was from a Genoese diplomatic mission to Ferdinand and Isabella congratulating the monarchs on their victory over Granada. Columbus' words are almost an identical translation from the Genoese letter which accompanied the diplomats. *Ibid.*, p. 135, note 27.

24. N. Cohn, *The Pursuit of the Millennium* (New York, 1970), pp. 310–314.

25. R. Southern, "Aspects of the European Tradition of Historical Writing: 3. History as Prophecy," *Royal Historical Association, Transactions*, 22, ser. 5 (1972), p. 173.

Index

133

Index

135

Index